2012
Meeting the Star Beings

The healing of humanity

Free Spirit

i

Acknowledgements

I would like to thank all the people who helped me and made this book possible. I am grateful for all the support from my friends and for the love of my family, and for every person who has ever played a part in my life, for they have all contributed in some way to bringing me to this point on my healing journey.

I also give thanks to the Star Beings, for entering my life and showing me the wonders of the Universe as well as showing me the reality of immortality and eternal love.

This book is an offering to humanity – may it bring healing, inspiration, understanding, love and light into the hearts of individuals planet-wide.

Free Spirit

Contents

Introduction   vii

Chapter 1
My personal journey   3

Chapter 2
2012 and Ascension   29

Chapter 3
Vibratory reality and healing   53

Chapter 4
Healing the fear   67

Chapter 5
Seeing through the illusions   87

Chapter 6
Toxicity and vibratory purification   103

Chapter 7
Meeting the Star Beings   125

Chapter 8
Entering into relationship with the Star Beings   149

Chapter 9
Glimpses of higher dimensions – alien worlds
and cities of light   171

Chapter 10
Humanity's healing crisis   193

Chapter 11
The new humanity takes shape – Open
Contact   215

Chapter 12
The star gates open   231

Chapter 13
The roadmap to healing   245

Chapter 14
The Plant Teachers   265

Chapter 15
Spiritual perspectives and reflections   279

Chapter 16
Closing messages – A call to action   287

Glossary   289

About the author   295

Introduction

Humanity stands at a crucial time in its evolutionary development. Having exceeded the carrying capacity of the Earth, our continued existence calls for and is dependent upon a radical transformation in consciousness. The answers to many of our problems lie in moving into a deeper heart space and by doing so we heal the separations and conflicts between us. We also open ourselves to the possibility of very deep healing and assistance from loving Higher Intelligences, who come now to guide humanity out of crisis and forth into the light.

Beyond this physical plane, lie realms of pure love and light, where higher dimensional beings from other star systems exist. These benevolent loving intelligences have transcended all sufferings, including death, and are thus immortals.

As we approach 2012, higher dimensional energies from the centre of our galaxy are streaming into the energetic aura of our planet, awakening our long dormant light bodies that many of us are not even aware we have. This is bringing our awareness into alignment with these higher realms and facilitating contact with these beings.

On the brink of extinction, humanity faces its greatest challenges and our spiritual task is now to draw in the loving and luminous vibrations of the higher dimensions, so as to bring about the insights and compassion needed to transform our consciousness, our hearts and our understandings of reality. This illumination in consciousness carries with it the potential to deeply heal our planet. With determination and an open heart, and the questioning of all we have been brought up to believe, we have the potential to heal all of our fears and come face to face with our true spiritual nature and be released from all suffering.

We then receive a massive healing on all levels and are then able to come out of our ego-created shells into the full light of the higher dimensional realities. We discover our own inner power and immortality, and are presented with the truth of a new reality of consciousness that has the potential to bring about a core healing in the heart of humanity.

Free from fear, we become deeply open in our hearts and we are then able to receive communication from the loving Higher Intelligences. We can then enter into relationship with them and receive their unconditional love, as we re-evaluate our identity and relationship with the cosmos. These intelligences come now to guide every one of us through this final healing crisis of humanity.

The ascension in consciousness will ultimately end all suffering in humanity, release us of all fear and awaken us to our immortal light nature if we allow ourselves to open and heal of our karmas, obscurations and defilements. The flowering of higher consciousness brings about the ability to see into realms beyond the physical and we are then presented with a Universe teeming with loving and wise intelligences. Star travel, portals to distant galaxies, a relationship with Extra Terrestrial Light Beings and an unbroken connection with the Divine Source all await humanity.

Physically, emotionally and spiritually we are currently only living to a fraction of our ultimate full potential. Constrained by fear, conventions and old habits, afraid to open our hearts to higher possibilities, we live in an illusion that this reality is all there is. With the courage and spiritual determination to free ourselves of all our fears and old conditionings, we realise that the physical reality is simply a thin surface level of a multi-dimensional ocean of consciousness. The deeper we voyage, the more of our old limited self we can transcend and we are then able to surrender into more expansive, loving and illuminated spaces. We will then find we have the potential to become superhuman simply by healing ourselves fully on all levels and so we can rewrite our current version of reality, becoming creators of our new future.

As we awaken into the new conscious possibilities, we will find that the old modes of consciousness are nothing other than a grand and elaborate fictitious story, created by the ego-self. Identification with this story is responsible for every single kind of suffering known to humanity. The new reality humanity has an opportunity to move into is one based on love and abundance where there are no limitations and where there is no fear or suffering.

The end of suffering comes when we become fully aware and fully loving human beings. We then rediscover our connection to the Spiritual Light, and our whole lives become fully aligned with the loving vibrations of the higher planes. Through a process of understanding, integrating, healing and opening our hearts we begin to find our way into these higher reaches of consciousness, guided by the Star Beings. In these enlightening and expansive realms of consciousness, we can discover the true depth and extent of love that is present in the Universe, and draw it into our being, so that we may become fully healed, and understand all the causes that have led us into this place of planetary crisis today.

Having healed our fears and orientated ourselves to the higher vibrations of love, as well as having cleansed ourselves of harmful bodily toxins we are then presented with new opportunities in conscious evolution. Previously inaccessible planes of reality will open up to us. The veils of death will collapse and we will be able to see into the afterlife dimensions whilst still alive, enabling us to recognise the truths of eternal life and immortality. The highest goal of the Ascension is to fully integrate the spiritual dimensions into our body whilst still alive and thus become immortal. Free from the shackles of death and rebirth, humanity can truly rediscover a more vibrant, wise and enlightened mode of existence. We always carried the seeds of this higher consciousness within our hearts but they became smothered by emotional and physical toxins. As humanity turned away from the Higher Love these seeds became unable to sprout and grow within our being.

However now as we have reached a turning point in consciousness having collectively done a lot of spiritual and transformative work, along with the grace and assistance of the Higher Beings, we can now turn toward the Light. The higher consciousness can then develop within our being, bringing with it the tools to heal ourselves and our planet, bringing back our remembrance of our cosmic origins and restoring our forgotten relationship with the Higher Beings.

We then heal the deepest separation and find that we are not anything other than an immortal super-conscious Light Being ourselves. Organised religion has created the illusion that we are separated from the Divine and we are not "God" or the "Divine" ourselves. This separation is deeply harmful to the heart of humanity and the spiritual reality is that we all can attain the Christ or Divine Consciousness and know the Divine directly. By healing this separation, we find inner empowerment, the fear that the organised religions have bred in us collapses and we become true masters of our own spiritual destiny.

When we are able to become channels of spiritual love then much can be achieved on Earth in a short time. It may well be that the structures of the old consciousness begin to collapse before the emergence of a widespread global consciousness of love and unity, but we should fear not, because only when we let go of the old can the new awareness really begin to come forth in humanity.

So, in this age of economic and environmental breakdown, there are messages of hope and love from the Higher Dimensions. These messages invite us to awaken and open our hearts, see beyond our self-created limitations and to embrace wider possibilities. The outer world always changes to reflect inner transformation and so as we begin to heal our fears and open our hearts, we will be presented with a new reality where love is predominant with the spiritual realities and truths becoming accessible to more of us.

In those spaces, our preoccupation with economic activities will diminish and love will become the driving force behind the evolution of our species. When we are open to love, we allow ourselves the possibility of entering into relationship with very wise and loving intelligences from other star systems who come to invite us to complete our healing and journey with them into their fantastic worlds of light cities, portals and conscious immortality.

This book will share some of my experiences with them and how we can move into a higher consciousness through healing and detoxification, with deep implications for the transformation and healing of humanity. This writing is an offering to humanity, so that more of us may realize the spiritual truths, recognise the vital importance of healing our fears and turn toward the Light before it does become too late for us.

Chapter 1

My Personal Journey

At the age of five, I remember looking up at the stars wondering what was out there and the meaning of such a huge universe. When I was six, I remember a journey up the M6 motorway in the UK Midlands and was presented with a vast vista of bridges, cities and huge pylons, far larger in scale than anything I had ever seen previously. A strange kind of consciousness then arose, where I realised it was simply all an illusion, a dream, created by the mind and the real reality was something far more mysterious and profound, now inaccessible to humanity because it had become caught up in this dream of fast cars, big motorways and tall buildings.

I remember that deeper consciousness being wordless, hyper-spatial and infinite, carrying within itself a vibration so loving and intelligent that nothing on the Earth could compare with it. As a child of six, I couldn't fully understand the implications of it, but I knew the ordinary world I had been born into was not ultimately real and there was a lot more to reality than what was before my eyes.

Weeks later, I was surprised one night to wake up to a banging sound and I found myself in some kind of space craft filled with golden luminescent light and beings in a circle banging some kind of metal drum filling my head with strange vibrations. That was the only experience of other-worldly beings I remember at that age.

At the age of 13, I was presented with the reality of human suffering and death, when my mother became seriously ill with a vicious form of liver cancer, killing her within months of diagnosis. This occurred after she had worked in a meat factory for two years and I always suspected the cause of this illness was due to the eating of vast amounts of processed pork pies, pasties and the like. It seemed so pointless to be born here, and die in suffering with no spiritual purpose. It was a painful experience, but when I was able to finally heal from it, I saw that all human disease and ultimately death itself are due to the choices we make. By healing unresolved emotional traumas and by living a healthier life on a physical and emotional level, we can avoid the necessity of such suffering.

I remember throughout my life many dreams of other-worldly places populated by strange beings made of light, who never ever got sick and did not even appear to age or die. It just seemed pointless for a human to come here for 70 years or so, and in some cases even less than that, and then die – on a stage with a backdrop of a cosmos 4.6 billion years old. There had to be some under-lying purpose and a continuation of life after death, or the accumulation of experiences here would have no lasting value. I often thought I did not belong on this planet, and somehow came here from elsewhere along with many memories of distant worlds, immortal beings, portals to other galaxies and the like. It was only much later in my life, at the culmination of 15 years of vibra-tory healing I was able to bring these memories into full awareness and begin to make some sense of them.

At the age of 21 I began to seriously take an interest in the spiritual life and began a long healing transforma-tive journey. Conventional and traditional Christianity, prevalent in my upbringing seemed to offer little in the way of answers to the biggest questions concerning our origins, spiritual purpose and relationship with the Universe.

After a brief immersion in Christianity as a teenager I came away from it with more questions than answers. It seemed strange to see people in worship, apparently following the commandments of God which prohibit killing and then seeing them feasting on a Sunday dinner of roast meat afterwards. Something seemed wrong. I also remember the teachings from the priests that because we were so inferior to God, that it was impossible to know God directly and it was necessary to go through the medium of Jesus Christ. I always thought that if there was a Divine Creator, it would surely be possible to have a direct experience of that intelligence, without having to go through another being or follow the rules set by an institution with its own agendas.

It soon became apparent that there was a lot of fear in Christianity and that people had taken up the faith because of a fear of eternal damnation in hell if they did not acknowledge Christ as the Saviour. I began to understand how this fear had been perpetuated by the leaders of the early Church in order to control and manipulate people into the faith. The increase in numbers served to empower the institution of the Church, whilst offering little in the way of spirituality for the individual. I wondered why with the messages of loving ones neighbour and not killing, there was so much global conflict and war due to religion.

I saw that underneath the surface of a religion promoting love and unity there was an underlying current of suppression, control and the hiding of deeper spiritual knowledge from the common people and this all had its roots in deep fear. Realising that this fear had done a lot of damage to humanity, closing our hearts and minds to a deeper more accessible spirituality and divorcing us from the possibility of a personal relationship with the Divine I began to search for alternative answers.

The summer of 1994 brought me to the experience of taking LSD, a powerful psychedelic. The first time I took it I became so afraid that I called an ambulance convinced I was going to die. I saw into a frightening different realm of consciousness beyond the body that seemed so familiar, yet I had never experienced it in this lifetime. Suddenly I had the awareness of the reality of an existence beyond the body and I saw that consciousness expanded beyond the confines of physical life. As the paramedics hooked me up to the cardiac monitor, reading a heart rate of over 186 beats per minute, I wondered if this strange mode of consciousness would ever pass.

Subsequent experiences with the LSD simply presented me again and again with a deep fear of death and an existential crisis, seeming to have no solution. Each experience, though touching me deeply on the heart level and teaching me much about the nature of reality - led me into many spaces where I felt the terror of imminent death. I soon left this path, finding no solution to the terror and fear presented to me and it was only many years later I learned that these experiences were reflecting back to me something I needed to resolve within myself – the fear of death. I was then drawn to the path of yoga and spirituality, to seek some answers to this existential crisis – that at any point I could die and there was nothing I could do about it.

In 1996, I left a conventional life of making a living from cooking in pubs and cafes, to visit the Himalayas where I spent months at a time in high altitude mountain villages. Here I came into contact with Eastern values and philosophies, notably Buddhism. Soon after the first trip to Nepal I renounced the eating of meat, seeing it as the cause of unnecessary suffering to animals. I also saw it as an environmental issue that humanity must face up to, to avoid a catastrophic food crisis in the future.

A deeper clarity of mind soon came about through meditation and the renunciation of the meat diet, though the issue of the fear of death remained unresolved. I took up mountaineering and developed a deep connection with the Earth, and it soon become apparent to me that humanity was seriously wrecking the eco-system in an attempt to acquire ever increasing levels of material wealth and comfort. The time high up in the Himalayas amongst snow capped peaks and Buddhist monasteries, showed me a more enlightening way of existence outside of conventional Western values which offered little in the way of spirituality.

I took up veganism (abstinence from all dairy and animal products in the diet) and very quickly began to enjoy a much healthier existence. By the turn of the millennium I realised that humanity could not possibly continue on the path it was on and often speculated on how much longer we actually had if we did not change. As I became deeply involved in the environmental movements, I realised how important it was for all of us to change our relationship with nature and to change our conventional notions of doing things, for they were clearly no longer working or bringing about any lasting happiness or meaning for humanity.

In the coming years as I experienced several different relationships, including one marriage, I realised how many humans hide from the existential crisis facing them by seeking comfort in a lifelong relationship with a lover. Though not intending to devalue the importance of human relationships, love, companionship and intimacy, it seems that they are given far too much importance and by getting too wrapped up in them one can lose sight of a higher spiritual perspective on life. The vision of marriage with children as a pinnacle of human existence, in the face of a human population that had exceeded the carrying capacity of the planet, seemed to offer little in the way of spiritual meaning and fulfilment.

On one late summer evening in 2003, I had a life changing experience with the psilocybin mushrooms, which at that time were still legal to buy from the alternative shops in Camden market, London. This was what first enabled me to experience the deep love that exists on other dimensions of being beyond our own. I experienced a profound ego-death experience that showed me the story of human life as simply a series of mental constructs and shimmering ideas, without any deeper substance in an expanse of infinite immortal consciousness. I came face to face with what back then I called God and felt the Divine love open up my heart on a very deep level. Though I was still very afraid of death, I was able to open my heart enough to be able to receive this healing love from the Divine dimensions. The conventional mindset is that these mushrooms cause temporary insanity, but it is my belief these medicines will ultimately prove to be the most valuable and healing to humanity, once the fears and misunderstandings around them have been resolved.

They enable us to see our life from a different perspective and offer us glimpses into dimensions beyond the physical life. Ultimately these medicines will help us to heal our fear of death, enabling us to open on a much deeper level and begin to understand the bigger spiritual meaning of human existence. Our existential issues can find resolution in the realisation of higher dimensional immortal consciousness and the realisation that the underlying energy of the Universe is that of love. It is the fear of death and the separation from a deeper cosmic love that keeps us closed to higher possibilities, trapping and binding us to this realm of suffering and mortality. We will need to heal our collective fear of death if humanity is going to make any serious spiritual progress.

The mushroom journey also brought me face to face with some deeply loving benevolent entities from another star system on a higher plane of consciousness. My fear prevented me from any deeper interaction with them at that time, but I was able to look up at the stars and realise that I had lived thousands, if not millions of existences on other worlds beyond space and time. I realised that Earth was not my home world, or the home world of many other humans, but this fact had been forgotten, lost in the entanglements of physical and material reality. I saw the potential for enlightenment, but I also saw humanity was wounded deeply by fear and a separation from the love of the Universe. I wondered how humanity could make it with so little time in environmental terms.

In 2004, after another visit to the Himalayas, I returned to the UK and changed my name to Free Spirit. I found it was very helpful in healing the old conditionings and jettisoning the old limiting beliefs so prevalent in society today that keep us separated from our true nature. The changing of the name proved to be a very powerful tool of transformation and gave me something to live up to, becoming totally free in spirit, free from fear and in a space of love and spiritual understanding. Though initially the name change brought up a lot of resistance in the people around me, later it brought about a healing in them, as it enabled them to face aspects of themselves that were challenged by the notions of freedom and a departure from convention. To this day I never regret the change of name, for though I love my family and have gratitude for them, I also see on a wider level it is necessary for humanity to move out of conventional ways of thinking if it is to survive long term.

I then spent several years involved in a Buddhist institution which in retrospect turned out to be built upon collective fear and the need to control people. However I learned a lot about meditation and experimented with chastity and came to some deeper spiritual realisations, as well as developing a deeper compassion and finding a strong connection to heart. It was at this time, my fear of death again resurfaced for resolution and whilst walking along the Suffolk coast one day came across a very old graveyard crumbling into the sea and was presented with the sight of human bones sticking out of the sand. This experience resulted in me being determined to heal the fear of death at its root and I then went on to visit a crematorium behind the scenes. This direct contact with death, dissolution of the elements and the experience of seeing human remains though very strong at the time brought about the beginning of the healing. This process began in the summer of 2007.

I spent a month in solitary meditation in the Spanish mountains the following winter and one night two weeks into the retreat I was visited by an angelic presence in the middle of the night, which I later named the Angel of Whitestar. For in the presence of this loving light my heart was able to open on a very deep level and the fear of death finally collapsed. In that collapse there was an explosion of love and the expansion of a wider consciousness. Bliss then arose, that rarely subsides even today several years later. I understood deeply that the fear of death acts as a stone cap on the heart and keeps us encapsulated in a space of fear, unable to move beyond the safety of the ego consciousness.

When we are finally freed of the fear of death, we are able to move forward into higher levels of conscious awareness and begin to perceive multidimensional realms of light and love beyond our ordinary reality. It is the fear of death and the denial of it that has contributed to bringing about so much suffering on the planet, which ultimately finds expression in humans killing one another in a vain attempt to escape from deep existential pain.

I left those mountains reborn in spirit and in heart and was able to see how institutions play on people's fears, for when one is free from fear, one is strong in oneself, and no longer needs to be involved in them. I moved away from the Buddhist group I was in and unfortunately legal issues prevent me sharing further details, though further on in the book I will discuss fear and control dynamics. These are widespread in society and not confined to one institution. When we are aware of these dynamics and heal ourselves, we cannot fall prey to any institution with dubious agendas.

Ultimately the deepest spiritual teachings can be understood and integrated without adherence to any kind of organised religion or belief system. The profundity of higher dimensional reality transcends all notions of ideas, concepts, dogmas, and belief systems. When we can experience deeply this spiritual reality we recognise Oneness, The Source, Illumination and Love. Any attempt to control or parcel up that Ultimate Truth into a belief system or religion immediately separates oneself from the experience of that Truth.

I began to work in nursing homes for the elderly and this work, albeit demanding at times, was a great teacher as I was able to develop a very deep sense of compassion for these people in suffering and coming to the end of their lives. It became apparent that most of these people were dying of diseases that had a root cause of unresolved emotional trauma and a build up of physical toxins in the body. Medical science has been busy trying to treat the symptoms of diseases but as yet has done little to address the underlying causes of disease, not acknowledging that toxins such as pesticides and heavy metals are a problem. I became aware that the majority of humanity carries an accumulation of harmful toxins in the physical body which keeps our hearts closed on a deeper level and prevents our spiritual faculties from working properly. Though this is not recognised by conventional medicine, personal experience of detoxification showed me unequivocally that the above is the case. If humanity wishes to receive spiritual illumination it will be imperative that these toxins cease to be used or ingested and are removed from the body. When they are, we can attain a much higher level of healing, to a point where we simply do not get sick. We then have no need for pharmaceuticals, doctors or hospitals. I do not engage with the NHS in any way and I now take responsibility for my own health and healing.

It was in late 2008, after being vegan for 15 years that I then took up the raw foods diet and the eating of only organic foods. The first few months were challenging, as the body sought to purge all accumulated toxins from the system, but I then moved into a state of perfect health. I had several mercury fillings removed, on concerns of toxicity and within a few weeks of having the mercury removed, began to experience a profound awakening in consciousness and the opening of the spiritual third eye. It seemed that the presence in my body of mercury had dulled my mental and spiritual functions. Free from mercury I discovered a deeper sensitivity of heart and a sharpness of mind never before experienced. At the same time I stopped drinking tap water, on concerns that fluoride and chlorine were having a similar effect.

In the summer of 2009, after a 15 year healing journey of body, heart and spirit, one day I became aware that my consciousness had deepened and taken on a multi-dimensional aspect. Turning it inwards, I was able to perceive infinite depth and one day several light beings appeared within the depths of my waking consciousness. These beings explained that they were trans-dimensional and exist in what we would call the dream plane. The dream plane is mostly subconscious, but with a purification of body and heart we can develop a deeper awareness and remembrance of dreams. Ultimately the boundary between sleep and waking is simply one of unconsciousness. In the higher dimensional conscious-ness the boundary is dissolved and one can access the dream/astral plane in waking consciousness.

At first, I thought I had imagined the phenomena but it repeated itself often. These light beings explained that humanity was facing societal and environmental collapse and had very little time to achieve a transformation in consciousness. They wished me to channel information from them to humanity as a whole about how to heal. These beings brought with them love from the other dimensions, that brought about an acceleration of my own healing processes and they also gave me the gift of foresight and increased intuition. I did notice that drink-ing more than a few glasses of tap water or eating non organic food would quickly stop this interaction from happening.

As the weeks went on, they began to take me on jour-neys during sleep to their star system which exists on a higher plane than ours. They explained that humanity will not be able to detect any signs of their civilisation, as they exist totally outside of our usual perceptual bandwidth and we will need to look within to make the contact. As non physical beings they are immortals and have transcended three dimensional space-time. I was gifted with being shown their cities of light, in other spheres of being, worlds ablaze with luminescence and colour, strange crystalline buildings and domes standing tall across alien vistas, with multiple suns and planets visible in the skies.

It was communicated to me that they have come in large numbers from other dimensions to help humanity with the planetary transitions. Ultimately, they come to assist those who wish to ascend out of matter entirely to drop the physical body and become conscious immortal light beings like them. They did stress that we are light beings like them too, but we have forgotten our true nature because of our birth into denser consciousness. I was shown their technologies, ranging from star gates and portals, to multidimensional star craft that had the ability to enter stars and utilise the gravitational energies at the core to emerge elsewhere in different parts of the galaxy. On occasions I was able to visit an even higher dimension where leaving a galaxy becomes possible through portal technology that utilises the intense energies present in the Galactic Core.

These beings showed me a profound love, which they also have for the whole of humanity. They bring with them messages and teachings for humanity so that we are able to make the evolutionary shift in consciousness. Sometimes my contact with them has brought an awareness of some aspects of myself in need of healing and has been challenging , but ultimately the relationship with them has been deeply transformative, as the extract from my personal diary illustrates;-

Entering into deeper relationship with the Star Beings is about giving up being in control and is a lesson in humility. A strong ego will either prevent contact altogether, or result in a very traumatic contact experience. Usually they will not initiate contact until an individual is ready. The lessons and initiations that they can instigate to bring about ones highest healing are not for the faint of heart. They will usually wait for people to have done a considerable amount of conscious personal healing, or spiritual work before coming forward and even then, we usually have to invite them. It is not that they want to harm us through creating difficult experiences, but they wish to teach us deep lessons in love, humility and self-surrender – and any difficulties experienced whilst we learn come from ourselves, our own unhealed aspects of our being.

Usually first contact brings about an expansion of consciousness and instigates personal transformation. For some people, contact goes as far as a couple of guided journeys into the astral plane, maybe seeing a couple of alien worlds and having a trip in a light ship, stopping there.

However if we want a much deeper relationship with the Star Beings, then we need to prepare to do some serious spiritual work. A full intimate relationship with the Star Beings requires total self surrender of ego, strength in heart and a determined spirit. As these beings are from the Higher Dimensions, we have to lose all of our fears. We have to lose our fear of death to be able to voyage into their realms, otherwise our consciousness remains identified with the body and remains bound to the lower planes.

If we can heal our fear of death, they will show us beautifully the reality of eternal life in a higher realm amongst the stars, communing with other deeply intelligent and loving beings. They can help us to see the possibility of transcendence of the human condition, which brings about a deep and unshakable liberation from the physical realm. We can still be in it, but we see it for what it is. It is just one mode of being, a temporary residence for learning and transformation. We will all leave it at some point whether we want to or not. We would do well to realise the impermanence of this realm. We may then fear that there is nothing for us if we let go of attachment to this realm. But this is our lesson, if we can let go and open up to the possibility of more, we will be presented with a much deeper, permanent and richer mode of existence.

A deep relationship with them will require us to transform anything that is negative in our hearts. For blocks in the heart generate distrust and fear, which are impediments to communion with them. Once we have made first contact, the love of the Star Beings enters into our heart bringing anything unresolved to the surface and instigating the final healings. We are guided in this healing journey by them. As we heal, surrender, and trust, they will show us more and bestow upon us more healing, confidence and empowerment, as well as guidance and clarity to bring ourselves into alignment with our highest purpose. Of course we have free choice, we are not obliged to enter into relationship with the light beings

- it is an invitation. But if we accept, we can receive very deeply and can begin the final spiritual work.

They show us a little at a time, guiding us toward the final goal - the Enlightenment. It is a gradual deepening of relationship with them, for otherwise it would bring up so much fear and unresolved issues that we would become totally overwhelmed and then not benefit. They show us as much as we can handle and then they step back, as then we often need to process or heal something. This is usually a deeper fear of transcendental reality, or a fear of moving beyond the ego. The relationship with them in my experience takes me to the absolute limit of consciousness, right out onto the leading edge, as far out of the comfort zone as they know I can handle. For this is where we can do the real spiritual work of transformation.

Only when presented with the total death of ego, in that scary and uncomfortable place, can we finally let go of our own petty stories, the illusion of I and our false notions of love. In that place it really feels like we have totally died and we are nothing, cast aside on some spiritual wasteland. The Star Beings hold this space of healing for us. We may not feel the presence of them in these moments for they cannot do our own work for us. They can hold a loving space, but we must discover our own true nature and do our own healing.

In the final crushing death of ego comes the surrender to Divinity. Then like a phoenix rising from the ashes of the old self we emerge into the Light and are remade with the immortal light of the Universe. A spiritual rebirth occurs and we feel the winged beings, the angels and the *light beings radiating their higher vibrations into our being. We feel the awakening of a deeper and enduring love for all of existence, the ego is transformed, we become one with the Universe, we rediscover and remember our true place in it and we find our true relationship with Divinity that we lost and turned away from. This is the final healing process, the surrender of ego, the letting go of self itself. The fires of compassion are then lit, we finally understand how things really are, we see through illusion and we can then become an instrument of transformation.*

This is the gift of deep relationship with these intelligences, the nurturance of ourselves by them as we begin our highest healing. The highest level of healing is to remember our cosmic origins, to rise out of confusion, to recognise ourselves as beings of Light and to reclaim our inner power. From here the castle of fear that has been built up within our being has been dealt a devastating blow and begins to crumble. Fear dissolves into feelings of love, compassion and forgiveness for others that are in fear and acting from that space. We can experience a very deep illumination and in this mode of consciousness we must enter into a total selfless service to the Divine. For now we have unleashed a dying beast from our consciousness, fear itself, frightened by itself and in its death throes it will attempt to thwart our return to the Light.

Hold to the Light, be humble, be totally humble, love with all your heart, surrender to the Divine, become an instrument of peace and then fear can no longer alight on any part of your being. Hold to this course and the dying beast of fear will dissolve back into the Light and be gone forever.

By this point we will have realised that we are an immortal hiding in a physical body pretending to be real down here in this illusory realm. There comes yet another invitation from the Star Beings – for we now have an invitation to leave this world behind and ascend, to go with them and be reunited with the Cosmic family of Star Beings. By completing our spiritual work, by being humble and being of service, we can resolve all of our karmas, be liberated from this realm of suffering forever and become a cosmic immortal. This is what lies at the end of the journey, this is why the Star Beings have come now, they come to invite us to awaken, transform, heal and return to the stars from where we came long ago.

The love and wisdom of the Star Beings is deeply profound and often I remember experiences with them in their star craft, totally humbled by the complexity and immensity of their technological achievements in those dimensions of being. At the same time, it is all built on love and in accordance with the Laws of the Universe. There is infinite energy available in the higher dimensions due to the operation of different laws of physics so they do not have issues with energy scarcity or competition for resources. To fully understand this, one needs to realise that hyper-spatial reality in a higher dimension is infinite and not separated from the intense energies from the Galactic Core. These realities are incomprehensible to us on this level but one day humanity will evolve to this level of intelligence.

I can only surrender and feel deep reverence for the love that emanates from these intelligences. When we

allow them to love us deeply, all of our fears are transmuted and released and our hearts open on a much
deeper level. My experience now is of having a beautiful,
deeply intimate and special relationship with these
beings. They have guided and nurtured me and helped
me in times of personal crisis to find my way back to
centre and to my life purpose.

In the summer of 2009, I was in a brief relationship
with a woman who was very controlling and abusive. As
I worked to extract myself from this relationship, having
experienced a considerable degree of auric and energetic
depletion, they appeared in my consciousness and instructed me to immediately go to Glastonbury Tor even
though it was 11pm. Upon making the summit of the Tor
in the darkness, then in my visual field a tall Star Being
appeared with a wand. It pointed out black energies
attached to my aura and a psychic black dagger had
penetrated my heart chakra and was depleting my
energy. This Being extended its wand and in a flash, all
these energies were dissolved and removed. In that
moment I received a full and total auric recharging and
healing. The Being then instructed me to go down and to
leave the relationship immediately.

Later the Star Beings were able to take me into their
realm and point out aspects of myself that were not
healed and that had led me into a relationship with this
person. With my permission, they were able to instantly
remove these defilements from my emotional body and
so I received deep relationship healing.

The implications of this are that if we are deeply open
to receiving from these beings and able to drop our fear

of them, they can help us to heal in so many ways which rapidly accelerates our spiritual evolution. They will show you anything within you that needs healing and then with their love you are assisted in healing yourself. All they ask then, is that you be of service to them, which means being of service to humanity. They have no other agenda than to help humanity to heal on the deepest level so that ultimately we can transcend the human condition as this writing taken from my personal journal below illustrates;-

I will share some of my experiences of healing from the Star Beings and explain why contact with them is so healing. The Star Beings are from higher dimensions, where they have transcended death and suffering. These higher realms scintillate and radiate pure love.

Our true nature is pure energy or cosmic vibration. Karmic issues and misconceptions about the nature of reality have resulted in our incarnation into a dense physical level of being. Most of humanity believing that this is the only reality, have invested all their energies into a reality that is subject to the laws of death, suffering and change. Thus we can never really be truly happy. At the same time our deeper connection is lost and we then lose the ability to receive healing communications from the Higher Dimensions.

Contact with the Star Beings is a lesson in trust, surrender and the letting go of fear. The Star Beings are infinitely loving and wise and have only our best interests at heart. To meet them we need to open our hearts and begin the work of raising our vibration. With an open heart and an open being, we can receive deep blessings from the Star Beings. They can transmit cosmic energies into our auras that can remove any blocks and bring about a massive healing. Then we can develop a very deep relationship with these Beings. These Beings are the teachers of humanity, ambassadors of Light from the stars and are loving and luminous immortals who come at this hour of need.

The heart of humanity desires awakening and so it will receive by the compassion of the Star Beings. Truth and justice will be restored to the Earth with the arrival of the Star Beings. It will herald the age of Enlightenment. From my own experience, ongoing contact with the Star Beings is a spiritual growth accelerator as we need to work and transform a lot to be able to have communication with and to receive from them. Once we have made the contact, they then facilitate the rest of the healing. Their love flows down from their dimensions like golden nectar poured down upon us from infinitely large jugs. There are few words that can describe these kinds of experiences adequately.

When they enter your life everything will open. Doorways to heavenly realms will open, the vibration of the body will speed up and you will become super-healthy, see into the future of your life and heal all of your personal relationships. You can become an instrument of love and healing for the benefit of others.

We can receive deep healing by being open to these higher dimensions. At first there may be fear as we feel presences and we suddenly see into the depths of space within our consciousness. The vastness and infiniteness of it all can be overwhelming but by trust and through surrender to the cosmic love we can incorporate these new realities into our being and receive transcendental nourishment which cleanses our soul on every level. At one point in my life I was afraid to talk to others suffering from deep blocks in the communication chakra. These Star Beings have nurtured me and given me deep healings so I can talk confidently to others and spread the word of the deep healing on offer to humanity from these loving intelligences. This I hope will deepen the collective understanding and show the way for others to find this healing.

This is what the new consciousness (The Ascension) is about, the incorporation of new realities into our being. Our outlook and vibration determines our reality. Within time the evolution of humanity will lead us to a point where we are able to let go of physical existence entirely. Our true nature is multidimensional and infinite. Our physical body is a dense shell that binds us to these lower realms. The loving emanations of the Higher Dimensions can heal our fears and heal our hearts. Fully healed, afraid of nothing, fearless and full of love, we are able to let go of self identity and the need to identify with the physical body. This speeds up our ascension process.

The Star Beings manifest now to help with the ascension of humanity. We too can ascend out of physical reality and be like them. This is the final healing for us. A fully healed vibratory being does not reside on the physical plane. Fully healed vibratory beings do not die and are at one with the Cosmos, able to travel beyond the stars and beyond this galaxy. The full journey is beyond our comprehension as there are many ascension processes during the cosmic lifespan of a vibratory being. The invitation of the Star Beings is to take the first few steps, to embrace infinite love, immortality and recognition of the Divine. They show us what we can be and what we will be. The possibilities are endless and the love they radiate knows no limits and can heal every single human heart on this planet.

The only thing that stands in our way of this massive healing is our fear. It is time to heal our fear as fear no longer serves us and keeps us closed to higher and more loving possibilities. Heal the fear in your heart and your soul and you will meet the Star Beings who will nurture you all the way to Ascension and beyond.

So the culmination of a long healing journey of eating only the purest foods and transforming my own inner fears and limitations has led to my life entering a very blissful space, filled with light and love and the celebration of a deep relationship with the Visitors. From these intelligences we are able to receive profound and complete healings on all levels if we are able to open our hearts to the possibility of relationship with them.

From them we can learn much about love and as our fears and self-imposed limitations are dissolved, we gain a deeper insight and understanding that can bring about powerful transformative change on this planet. Even when all seems hopeless, even at the eleventh hour for humanity, much can be turned around and healed through an orientation of the heart toward spirit. It is the attachment to ourselves and our own dramas that keep us closed to the expansiveness that exists beyond the boundaries of the ego self and it is this expansiveness we so urgently need to discover now.

When we do, we see beyond ourselves, beyond the small story of our own lives, we see the bigger picture – six billion humans all separated from connection with one another and the Divine Source. In this place, how can there be peace, harmony and common understanding?

The healing of humanity and the damage we have done to our environment can only be brought about by the transcendence of this fragmented collective consciousness into a unified loving and conscious whole with single common purpose. There is great hope for humanity now, but it calls for each and every one of us to make the transition from fear to love and to heal ourselves on many levels so we are able to live up to the challenge of bringing in the new consciousness. The healing we all need to do if we wish to make the ascension in consciousness is discussed in later chapters, but firstly an overview of the 2012 consciousness shift is called for.

Chapter 2

2012 and the Ascension

Many writings portray the 2012 date as being 'the end of the world' or prophesying some apocalyptic event for humanity. I believe this is a manifestation of fear and does nothing to help heal our fears, which is required for us to move into higher consciousness. Indeed humanity does have some very serious issues, both environmentally and socio-economically and there may be some regional breakdowns or disasters. However a total annihilation or destruction of humanity is unlikely and I believe what the 2012 prophecies point towards is the death of the old modes of consciousness and the associated structures.

The scale of any disaster or environmental breakdown will be dependent on how resistant or open we are to making changes. It is required for humanity to re-evaluate its relationship with the Earth and the Universe as well as with one another if we are to survive. For some this statement is enough to make them retreat in fear back into their comfort zones. However the reality is that we all need to look at our fears and actions and re-examine our views on reality, letting go of false views and beliefs that impede and harm us so as to contribute to the wellbeing and continued existence of humanity.

There is I believe a difference between propagating fear for its own sake and raising an awareness of issues that humanity needs to become conscious of. The first is harmful, however the later is helpful in that it presents us with an opportunity to move out of denial and fear, see the truth of our situation and begin to work on those patterns and behaviours that are not conducive to harmony and challenge the long term ability of humanity to remain on Earth sustainably.

All manner of behaviours that humanity are currently engaged in are harmful to our long term wellbeing and thus the arising of the light consciousness will call for us to look again at these actions, so as to make conscious changes or to renounce those systems that do not serve humanity. Some examples in need of urgent reform or abandonment include the attachment to exponential growth economies, the banking system, political corruption, imbalances of wealth, nuclear proliferation, organised religions, the eating of meat, inorganic farming, mercury toxicity, continued use of fossil fuels, animal experimentation, the medical system, our views of love and relationships and the suppression or manipulation of spiritual truths by religious or political institutions.

All of the above, as well as more not listed, clearly do not serve humanity and yet are still prevalent in human consciousness. It is the world created on these values and systems that will collapse from 2012 onwards, rather than the whole of humanity itself. For those still attached to the values of fear, control, manipulation and excessive consumption and resistant to change, the coming years will bring forth a lot of difficulty and suffering as the old consciousness begins to collapse. For the structures that are not based on truth, light, compassion and universal understanding must give way to allow a renaissance of spiritual consciousness on the planet.

It is likely that 2012 will spell the end of the current economic age as the economy has simply grown so monstrously large, that it cannot be sustained without the total plundering and consumption of all natural resources. No world leader has yet had the courage to stand up and acknowledge that the economic system must be abandoned and replaced with a sustainable love based economy and immediately. It will be a difficult lesson for humanity, but a necessary one, for if we do not voluntarily reduce economic growth, nature will force the issue – with the potential for significant human population reductions as the infrastructures and resource pools collapse.

It is this unsustainable economy underpinned by dependence on fossil fuels that has artificially raised the carrying capacity of the planet. With oil reserves dwindling and no realistic replacements as yet, humanity is very close to this scenario of some degree of population contraction. Only a mass spiritual awakening that brings awareness to our actions can turn the situation around. Solutions to our energy crisis can be found in higher consciousness. The external energy crisis is a manifestation of our inner disconnection to the spiritual Source. When we discover this connection within, I believe new sources of unlimited energy will become manifest in the physical plane which will liberate humanity from this era of energy scarcity.

For those who have already worked through their attachments to the old ways of being, 2012 marks the beginning of an age of great promise and spiritual enlightenment. For those who choose the new way of love, unity, peace and spiritual illumination, their lives will become filled with ever increasing levels of love and abundance. New structures built on spiritual values will flourish post 2012 as a wave of enlightened conscious-ness begins to spread throughout humanity. For these individuals, suffering will become a thing of the past as their lives will be lived in full alignment with the Spirit, and their ascension process will be well underway. At any time each individual has the free choice to choose their destiny, however those choosing the old ways will be subconsciously drawn there because of unresolved karmic or emotional issues in need of resolution before they are able to embrace higher consciousness.

Astronomically, 2012 is a significant date as the Solar System has entered briefly into a higher dimensional photonic beam of energy radiating outward horizontally from the Galactic Core. This happens every 26,000 years, and the passage takes around 10-15 years to complete. During these times of Galactic plane transit, the Earth and Sun become energized by higher dimensional vibra-tions being emitted from the Galactic Core. This has the effect of raising the energetic vibration of the Solar System and boosting our auras, thus accelerating the resolution of any inherent blockages. This influx of higher dimensional energy will instigate a thorough vibratory purification of ourselves and the Earth.

For those attuned to these higher vibrations, it is possible to receive communication from intelligences on higher planes. These communications often contain instructions on how to heal everything unresolved within and then how to orientate one's life in service to human-ity. These higher vibratory communications in the ap-proach to 2012 will be available to more individuals as they heal their hearts enough to push their conscious awareness into these new bandwidths of consciousness.

At the same time 2012 marks a point where the Earth intersects higher dimensional fields of energy. The effect this will have is that previously invisible beings on other dimensions will become visible to a large section of humanity. The prelude to this is receiving the communications through consciousness and / or telepathically. The reason why humanity has not experienced a mass visitation recently by Star Beings is because there has been a perceptual rift in consciousness and the star gates (inter-dimensional portals) have been closed up to now. We also need to be vibrationally attuned and healed deeply on the heart level in order to be able to have contact with them, for otherwise it would be too traumatic for us. However as we approach 2012 and the consciousness of humanity rises, then the possibility of mass open contact with these benevolent and loving beings becomes possible.

Ascension in these writings refers to the movement from one sphere of consciousness into another. There are many different forms of Ascension but they all have the same underlying characteristic of conscious movement between planes of reality or consciousness. The first type of Ascension that we are already seeing in some of humanity is of movement out of purely materialistic and egotistical consciousness into spiritual and loving realms of consciousness. As a sentient being makes a conscious shift upwards, the external reality then changes to match the inner state. Thus one's life can become free of suffering, more guided and more illuminated as one makes the shift. Things that no longer serve are released and new creative energy emerges in one's life bringing about deeper expression, meaning and direction.

This is only the first step on the journey of Ascension, for when one has become more established in these spiritual spaces of existence, then more possibilities open up for further Ascension. It will become apparent that after one has worked with the fear of death, portals into other dimensions exist within ones consciousness. When they have been discovered, or more correctly, brought into conscious awareness, then it is possible to make astral journeys into them and emerge from there into luminous higher dimensional realities as another extract from my journal depicts;-

The first thing that will strike any astral plane visitor in this realm is the fluidity and mobility of movement and the light vibrations. This dimension is the realm of Light. At first one may think they have become at one with God or the Source, however the light emanations are only the effervescence of the Source, rather than the Source itself. There are many stages on the journey beyond even this dimension that take us through the Galactic Core, into the realms of liquid light and upwards toward final unity with Source.

In the fifth dimension we meet ethereal beings (angels, devas and nature spirits). We also meet the Star Beings who mind the dimensional portals as well as engaging in activities that are conducive to the evolution of humanity as well as living out their highly evolved and interstellar existences.

In this dimension the transmutation of the body has occurred leaving behind the carbon based form and is replaced with a light-based crystalline structure of a

much finer and subtler vibration. The biological structure has been considerably transformed so that it can
handle the light vibrations. Thus some inhabitants of
this realm, including many ET races, can live on planets
in multiple sun systems. Beings on one of these worlds
over a lifetime of a minimum of several thousand years
would witness anything up to 25 seasons spread over
decades as up to five suns complete complex orbits
around one another. At times several suns would rise
together casting utter brilliance across their world and a
brightness that would destroy the biological structure of a
three dimensional being. Hence the three dimensional
body needs to be transmuted and the denser vibrations
relinquished before one can come here permanently.

Everywhere and everything in this vibration is guided
by the Law of One – the recognition that all stems from
the same source. Duality, fear, hatred, suffering and
ignorance along with a range of other negative aspects of
personality are gone. There is still a subtle sense of individuality, however all entities here understand deeply
and live according to the Law of One and are able to
emanate unconditional love, for they realise they are all
aspects of the same Whole.

Up here there are huge collectives and groupings of
Star Beings. Here we realise our true light nature, we are
spiritually awake and a sense of long lost familiarity
returns. Our long slumber in lower dimensional reality
has ended and we now exist in peace, joy, expansiveness,
light and endless vitality. The lower dimensions are
visible below us. Many light beings are working in this
realm for the ascension of those below. Depending on our
vibration, above us we may perceive even higher realms.

From here we can see far into multidimensional space and just with an intent or wish we may see alien worlds or star systems light years away in ordinary reality.

The notion of distance that creates so much spatial separation on the lower realms is transcended. Interstellar travel is normal up here. From here the other purpose of stars becomes apparent. Streams of light beings are entering as well as emerging from stars as stars are huge vortices of light which form inter-dimensional gateways. In this dimension one can fly into a star and emerge from another. This is usually done through the use of hyper-spherical spacecraft that can utilise the energies of the star to affect dimensional travel. The expanse of this realm is virtually limitless and beyond ordinary comprehension.

Here, depending on our wishes we can commune deeply with Star Beings and explore the galaxy which encompasses millions of inhabited spheres, each the residence of unique collectives of star races all with unique purposes. These are all invisible and undetectable to ordinary inhabitants of Earth as there is a perceptual rift separating them. Star systems that look barren from Earth can actually host Star Beings on the higher dimensions – and a star system exists across a continuum of multidimensional reality. A single star can paradoxically host several ET races simultaneously as dimensions can exist intertwined with one another, yet remain perceptually distinct from each other.

A whole array of eight dimensional beings could be living on a brane world (dimensional membrane) intersecting the Earth and our bodies and we would never know about it as the vibrations are so fine they exist in the 'gaps' in our vibrations. Multidimensional reality is complex and multifaceted and we of the third dimension are not able to see the 'gaps' in our denser vibrations to see the simultaneous realities beyond. The gap between the dimensions is microscopically small, yet we cannot perceive these other realities if we are not vibrationally attuned.

After some time becoming familiar with the Middle and Upper Astral Planes (the fifth and sixth dimensions) one will become aware there is a dense barrier between this reality and the astral planes blocking full remembrance of the higher planes. This is not the ordinary condition of humanity, to be separated in this way from the higher planes, but rather a temporary condition we are experiencing as a result of our descent into lower planes of consciousness which is exacerbated by the poisoning of our pineal gland (spiritual third eye) by heavy metals and pesticides.

The spiritual work for us now is to deepen our awareness and cleanse our bodies of harmful toxins. This will then dissolve this barrier of unconsciousness and create a reverse movement back up through the planes of higher consciousness. When we do this our dreams will become far more lucid and the notion of sleep will change as we become able to lie down in bed and with full consciousness move across into the other planes. This will rapidly accelerate our spiritual development as we will be able to draw in and integrate far more information and communications from the higher planes which is usually forgotten upon awakening.

When we begin to dissolve the barrier between the worlds, much bliss can arise in our hearts as we become able to receive the love from the higher planes and in some instances to meet the Star Beings themselves. The following notes from my log illustrate the experience one can have and describes the resulting influx of love into one's being;-

On our journeys toward the final ascension we may notice that between the physical and astral plane there is a significantly thick barrier. This barrier makes it very difficult to make a fully conscious bridge between the two worlds, which ultimately are one world. However our dualistic consciousness has created the reality of them being separate worlds and thus created this barrier between them. As this barrier dissolves, ones being may well gravitate more toward the astral planes than the physical and thus one feels an upward movement of awareness within ones being.

One of the way-stages to ascension is the dissolving of this barrier so that one can be fully conscious of the astral plane whilst awake. This is a rare experience to have and if we have it we should try and cultivate it further. When this occurs it may feel like the top of the head has suddenly opened up into some vast conical structure and at the same time as perceiving the usual three dimensional world around us we can see far into 'astral space'. We may have visions of spirits or other beings, or of alien worlds with fantastic landscapes. One may have the experience of suddenly surfacing from some 'sea' into a scintillating or expansive landscape, like a dolphin jumping out of the sea into the light.

We may suddenly feel overwhelmed with beautiful emotions along with the awareness of being surrounded by hundreds of light beings. We can become aware and conscious of the unconditional love that these angels or light beings bestow on us. This kind of love is healing as it heals our hearts on a deeper level. We can then turn to our families and loved ones and love them in a deeper and richer way, whilst a flowering forth of forgiveness can arise for those who have wronged us. The potential for transformation of the heart through experiencing their love, is a very beautiful gift that these Light Beings offer to us.

In one experience;-

All of a sudden above the head everything became vacuous, like empty space. There was some inverted cone extending upwards and a multitude of sensations poured forth from above. I sensed star systems and alien worlds, light beings and angels.... And then there was pure bliss and a flowering within the heart as some divine love came through my being like some kind of heavenly nectar. I felt cleansed on a deep level, filled with joy and then I realised the value of the experience.

My mind turned toward humanity and the current situation. As a species we are consuming and poisoning our planet, have turned away from the Law of One and are at war with one another as a whole. The Beings conveyed the message "talk, go forth and share these experiences with humanity".
I felt a deep surge of love for the whole of humanity even for its darker parts still in fear, conflict and separation. I

saw how the energy of the Earth was increasing and as a result we are being propelled higher towards ascension and spiritual awakening and these Beings have come to assist us.

As mentioned earlier, the dissolving of the physical / astral barrier is a way-stage on our path of ascension. From here on we can develop a full astral mobility enabling us to consciously move around the astral, purposefully and with clear intent. We can also share and receive information whilst doing so, as well as developing relationships with other astral inhabitants and Star Beings, many of whom are from dimensions beyond the astral. We can work toward this by aspiring to become lucid and aware in dreams and during sleep. If we find ourselves aware we are dreaming we are on the astral plane. One should take care not to wake up and practise moving around the surroundings so as to enhance memory and dreamscape awareness. In one dream experience;-

I ran down a road toward a cliff and leapt off and landed on some grass. I suddenly 'woke up' in the dream. The urge to wake up properly was strong but I resisted. I stood up and took stock. I was aware of how real everything was. I patted the ground, touched the grass, felt the solidity of the earth and it was in no way less real than the ordinary world. There was no way to tell it apart, save for the knowledge I had a body sleeping elsewhere. I was fully present, awake in that place and in that moment I decided to start wandering around and looked up to see a huge volcano venting out masses of green smoke. The thought arose it would be interesting to go and fly up and check out the smoke. There the memory is lost.

So part of the process of Ascension is to develop a deeper lucid awareness of the dreamscape, for these territories are actually higher dimensional realities that we can explore in depth. We will find these realms often contain strange but familiar landscapes and this indicates that we were once far more familiar and connected to these higher vibratory realities. When we are able to consciously dream, we can then navigate through these realms and begin to have some conscious interaction with the inhabitants. Then we soon become aware of the reality of Higher Beings up there with an interest in our wellbeing and development.

Indeed the dream-world should be the first place for humanity to look for signs of extra-terrestrial intelligence (intelligence beyond the Earth plane). When it does look here and explores with an open mind and heart, what it will be presented with will be far beyond anything currently imaginable. The dreamscape is a portal to yet other realms and with a little training one can find portals to distant corners of the galaxy and one can even move beyond the astral plane.

Here, in the dream-world we meet the Star Beings – The Guardians of Humanity and when we can fully understand their messages we discover that they have already made the full Ascension and reside permanently on those realms. They can teach us that we too have the opportunity to enjoy an existence on the non-physical planes, free of a physical body, free from death and suffering if we so wish. So the second type of Ascension, is about departing from the human condition, and dropping the physical body. However the Higher Beings also teach that this can happen without having to die but rather through a process of bodily transmutation, by raising the consciousness of the body to the point where matter can become light. The completion of that process marks the passage out of the human condition and we become a conscious immortal light being.

We are in this Earth dimension now to learn lessons about how to live and how to love and to resolve some old stories and to recognise our true nature. Completing all of this earns us passage onwards out of the Earth dimension. We can choose to remain to help others if we wish but once our pre-agreed mission here is completed then it is time to leave. Ordinarily human life ends through death but every 26,000 years there exists an opportunity for Ascension without dying if we can attain the necessary vibration. This is done by bodily and emotional cleansing as well as through spiritual practice and the development of compassion and love.

With 2012 approaching we are all now suddenly being lifted up into higher vibratory realities. The consequence of this is a massive cleansing and purification period for humanity as many blockages come to the fore at once for resolution, for unresolved issues cannot remain unresolved if we are to ascend higher. This offers the potential for great healing for many of us and the healing involves a cellular reconstruction of the body which results in a permanent increase in vibration and the establishment of new realities. The new realities are of abundance, peace and joy, the absence of suffering and the perception of previously invisible realms. We may become able to see the star beings or angels, along with a whole host of other multidimensional phenomena.

2012 and the Ascension

For those who are resistant to the healing their reality will remain the same but their lives will become more challenging and chaotic as their bodies are unable to assimilate the energies from the Galactic Core. Surrender and healing is possible at any point, but for those that choose not to embrace the ascension they will notice another sector of humanity beginning to speak of new realities, of light, of angels and other worlds that they have no comprehension of. Afraid and in refusal to allow the healing they may begin to strike out at the ascending ones, though with little success, for the ascending ones are well protected by the Higher Beings.

The Earth can support a being with a vibration falling within a particular range. For those able to complete their personal healing and resolve all their karmas, as well as being able to integrate the quickening vibrations from the Galactic Core, a point will come where further movement up the vibratory scale is not possible whilst on Earth. Post 2012, these people will have two options, they may either remain as they are on Earth to help others or continue the journey upwards in which case they will leave the Earth through a portal and the spirit has then completed its work here.

The Earth contains many portals (star gates) to higher dimensions that are hidden to us as we are not yet vibrating highly enough to be able to see or use them. The portals are energetically sealed requiring a certain level of vibration to access them. The ascendees once they have attained the vibration necessary can in an instant leave the Earth. Someone remaining would simply observe the person to vanish before their eyes, although they would have become translucent and radiating rainbow light in the run up to their disappearance so it may not come as a total surprise.

They will not have died, but their body will have become transmuted and light enough to move into a higher dimensional planetary system of which there are many. In fact they will have transcended death and have become an immortal free from the cycle of birth and death. Toward the end of 2012 the first wave of Earth departures will occur. For those remaining, those of a medium vibration will be able to assist in the work of transforming and healing the Earth and assisting those of lower vibration. However the increase of the Earths vibration will have resulted in a change in the vibratory bandwidths of beings that it can support. Thus those of the lowest vibrations will not be able to remain on Earth and if still resistant to healing and transformation will have to leave through death, being reincarnated elsewhere to continue their evolution - overseen by the Star Beings.

For those able to vibrate out of the Earths frequency field there is the promise of immortality as well as contact with a wide array of higher dimensional Beings from numerous planetary systems spread across the higher dimensions, undetectable to us here. The Earth departing spirits will also ease to some extent the looming population crisis. It may well be that the surge in human numbers is due to the amount of souls needing to incarnate here, to learn final lessons in preparation for higher dimensional existence beyond the Earth.

As 2012 approaches, the population will separate out into three groups, those who will be able to leave Earth for a higher dimension of existence, those who can stay and transform the Earth and humanity, and those that will have to leave for an alternative realm to continue their karmic lessons. Naturally the first is the most favourable. This is achieved by resolving all ones karmas, surrendering to the highest healing, letting go of this reality and being open to new realities as well as opening ones heart to receiving the love from the higher dimensions.

Be compassionate to those who may not be able to make this journey but do not let them compromise your life mission and thus stop you ascending. Above all, move beyond all your fears, for it is fear that saps our vibratory energies and keeps us locked into suffering and separated from the Source. Once your personal healing reaches a point where leaving the Earth is an option for you there will come a day where you will know without doubt that the ascension process is well under way as this writing from my internet blog illustrates;-

At some point on the personal journey one will find that one's vibration suddenly accelerates and brings about massive changes in one's life. Things will start to happen very quickly, as wave after wave of higher dimensional energy is drawn into the being and assimilated. The Earths energy grid is now rapidly accelerating in frequency and so we are being propelled into high frequency states - being able to integrate this vibration brings about healing and awakening.

As this happens one may experience a deep bodily healing and transformation. Every single cell in the body will become supercharged and the whole being will be-

come lighter and springier. The body may shake involuntarily, releasing stored tensions. The need for sleep will rapidly drop off as one will be able to do more assimilation of daily experiences whilst awake. The distinction between dreams and waking will become obsolete as one becomes aware of the multifaceted nature of consciousness and numerous bridges of awareness will manifest where once there was a murky impenetrable veil. Dreams become clear, sharp and radiant and have a full meaning totally congruent with ones daily experience. This is a sign of energetic seals within the body energy matrix dissolving and with a free movement of energy between the waking and the astral there is a full recollection of experiences in the higher realms.

It will become apparent that the dream world is not something distinct and separate from our daily reality, but rather it is an extension of our multidimensional nature which exists across many realities simultaneously. Ascension calls for the integration of all of these different realities into our current awareness. There may be the experience of time dilation, the ability to see snippets of the future and an increase in the number of prophetic dreams. Following this, one can develop the ability to know the future of one's life.

Interesting things begin to happen to our spatial perception. Holes and rips begin to appear in three dimensional realities and one begins to experience super-consciousness and the ability to zip through portals in space time. There may be the experience of being elsewhere in the Universe, on other worlds. All this can happen in an instant as the higher realities transcend time. Linear perception then dissolves into a hyper-sphere *of multiple simultaneous realities where one can interact with several at a time.*

As these changes occur it is important to remember to trust the process and not be afraid even though there may be little in the way of external reference points to give any kind of assurance or explanation for what is happening. The memory of the multi-dimensional nature of existence is returning to us and is being drawn down into our current reality, totally rewriting it and quickly.

Duality begins to dissolve into an ever expanding sense of Oneness, resulting in conflicts of mind and heart dissolving and collapsing into the eternal centre of ones being. One can begin to feel the finer vibrations entering one's being, often descending through the crown chakra, resulting in increases in energy, psychic sensitivities and wellbeing. Sometimes the surges in energy seem too intense and almost uncontainable, and it seems the whole being will be totally overcome with it. It is important to keep ones ground to earth in some way so as to be able to keep assimilating the new energies. This process is going to speed up even more over the coming years.

The extra energy being integrated will result in increased mental function, which will enable you to make the right decisions in a rapidly changing external environment. It will be necessary to protect your energies from those who display fear and resistance to the ascension process by maintaining distance whilst remaining compassionate. As your own fear dissolves, your compassion will deepen dramatically.

At some point you will begin to near the crossover stage. Crossover is when you begin to transition from being rooted in three dimensional realities to being more established in higher dimensional states. Both realities will exist simultaneously as we near crossover and at some point the three dimensional reality will disappear altogether for those choosing to leave the Earth.

By this point you may well have had some contact with Star Beings or other spirit guides. They are helping and assisting you with the final healings needed to ascend. They are your teachers and as we begin to trust, we can learn deeply from them. They will teach you lessons of humility and surrender. Any reinforced notions of self will be totally obliterated with a deep contact experience, resulting in what may be a very difficult and shocking ego-death experience. However if we accept the teachings in this experience, the Star Beings will remake us in a different way. We may have the experience of being visited by nature spirits and devas, fluttering around ones being, gently restoring energy to us in a loving and deeply touching way after a difficult ego-death experience. This can be very deeply healing as they are assisting with the transformation of the body into light form.

If you consent, the Star Beings from the Higher Dimensions will help your ascension by beginning a series of initiations into multi-dimensional reality. One may have the experience of temporarily moving into their realm, seeing light ships, portals, and a wide range of other fantastic and strange technologies existing in the finer vibrations above the physical. They may also do body healings on you so as to lighten your vibration further for bodily ascension.

One day there will come a point where you realise your time on Earth is drawing to a close. Remembrance of your cosmic origins will return and the realisation will come that you once had a deep connection with the Universe, traversed the distances between the stars in Light ships and had deep relationships with a huge collective of Higher Intelligences. The time here on Earth was only ever meant to be a temporary one, we never originated here, rather we chose to come here for specific purposes and forgot our origins when we incarnated. Some of you may become aware you were sent here by the Star Beings to come and help humanity.

Soon so much energy will become manifest in your being which will enable you to see and potentially use the exit portals. It is a difficult notion for many people to comprehend, but our vibrations are rising to the point of being able to vibrate off the Earth. This farfetched notion will become reality as the possibility of it manifests right before us. If we manage not to succumb to fear and continue raising our vibration, three dimensional reality will no longer exist for us and so we will literally disappear off the planet to continue existence in the Higher Dimensions free from suffering, sickness, death, anxieties and a whole host of other afflictions that trouble us in this reality.

Earth departures by spirits through ascensions are a normal part of the cosmic cycle. History tells us advanced civilisations succumbed to war, famine, or other catastrophes. Occasionally they did, but in most cases they simply realised that reality is multidimensional and that other planes of existence lie above this one, so they opted to leave for the higher planes and immortality, returning to the stars from where they came.

Chapter 3

Vibratory reality and healing

The reality we experience depends on our inner state of being and we all 'vibrate' at a particular level of consciousness. The particles of our body on the quantum level are ultimately packets of vibrating energy and science has shown that all matter has a dualistic nature – being both a wave and a particle at the same time. The amount of energy the particle has will determine which aspect is emphasised. There becomes a point where a particle can vibrate at such a high frequency, that the wave/particle duality is transcended and the particle ceases to be matter and is simply wave. People able to achieve this within their bodies can ascend off the Earth.

At a very low energetic frequency, the particle aspect is most dominant and matter takes a far more solid, dense form. The new consciousness that humanity is experiencing is occurring because the particles of our body are becoming highly energised and thus are able to become less dense and move more toward the wave aspect of matter.

When we become less dense energetically, we feel wellbeing, happiness and a free flow of energy. The body functions well and the heart is open. This will then result in the manifestation of an outer reality which as a reflection of oneself is far more harmonious, abundant, alive and vibrant. We can change our outer reality and experience by healing our energetic blockages within. Blockages are pockets of dense matter, a coalescence of old toxins in the body that lead to stagnation. In these spaces, negative emotions can also become stuck and if we are not able to clear these inner blockages, outer reality will again mirror our inner reality. We will then experience being stuck in our lives, experiencing frustration and then further negative outer experiences such as disharmony, conflict and lack of love will become manifest.

So we can become architects of our own reality. As we heal our physical and emotional blockages, there is a freer movement of energies within the body and our overall energetic vibration increases. The higher dimensional realities are far more energetic in nature, so for us to be able to perceive and interact with them we need to increase the energetic frequency (vibration) of our bodies. The healing of dense blockages is thus a very powerful tool for the transformation of our consciousness and our reality. If we are in a space of fear, suffering or difficulty, it will be an outer mirror of some aspect of ourselves in need of healing. If we are able to develop an awareness and willingness to look at parts of ourselves that need healing, we can transform those parts of ourselves and experience a rise in our level of conscious vibration.

There will come a point on this vibratory journey where once we have cleared all of our unresolved emotions and worked to clear the energetic channels in our body through yoga, we will move out of all suffering. Suffering is a characteristic of lower vibratory realms and can be transcended simply through resolving the blockages responsible. When we become blocked, we become attached, unable to release or receive and we become resistant to healing. These negative states keep us closed on the heart level and resistant to the free flow of energies from the Higher Dimensions which ultimately carry with them the ability to heal us of every-thing.

The deeper reality, of which most of humanity is not aware, is that a fully healed vibratory being does not reside in this three dimensional world of suffering, death, and limited energy. The rewards of healing our-selves fully are the ability to transcend all suffering and fear, to tap into a higher dimensional field of limitless spiritual energy and to receive an abundance of love. We can then begin to integrate the higher dimensional modes of consciousness. When taken to a high level we can even transcend death and become immortalised. Our dreams become richer and we can discover portals in the dreamscape to other worlds of light, populated by im-mortals. When we go there with our astral bodies we can bring back with us much information to assist in the healing of ourselves and humanity. The ultimate reward for healing ourselves on every level is that once we have become consciously immortalised, we can leave the physical realm entirely – without dying. We have the option to ascend into a higher dimensional plane of existence where suffering is no more.

We all carry the seed of immortality but as most of us are unaware of it, we are not able to integrate the reality of immortality into our lives, so we become vibrationally and energetically bound to this dimension and thus have to experience continual rounds of rebirth and death. If we are able to align all of the particles in our body to the energies of a higher dimension and remove all attach-ments to this one, the energy of spirit can flow through us unimpeded and in that moment our physical body becomes transmuted into spirit. We become a light being, free of the physical body and are then able to leave for a different dimension. A vision of these higher dimensions is depicted in the following writing – an extract from my personal log;-

Light cities exist up here with incredible radiance and beauty, constructed to focus energy through from higher dimensions, to magnify it and direct it elsewhere. This entire level is created from Light Consciousness and can host any being attuned and receptive to it. The purpose of existence up here is Love, celebration of limitless expansiveness and being an instrument of Oneness. We can relate to one another up here in much deeper ways. The self protective mechanisms of the lower dimensions are gone. We are just vibration up here and we naturally attract like vibrations. Love is everywhere as it is the underlying energy of the entire realm. Everything sparkles with its own innate beauty, coming forth from its Divine blueprint.

Nature is so much more varied up here, as are the colours and intricacies, as the Divine manifests itself in so many ways in this dimension. Though there is no solid form, there are many subtler ethereal forms up here. Many beings are composed of rainbow light and are almost transparent. Contact with these rainbow entities is very deeply healing to the heart and spirit, purifying our hearts of negative emotions through the experience of their love. They can help us to expand our hearts to become more loving on the Earth plane and thus speed up our karmic healing processes.

The vibration of this ascended realm is pure and clean as all parts of the being not attuned to the Light are gone.

Darkness and associated behaviours are a result of parts of ones being that have become blocked and resistant to the Light. Here we review our previous existences in lower dimensions and often feel remorse, for we see with an enlightened wisdom how our negative behaviours stemmed from our misunderstandings of reality and a forgetting of the Law of Oneness. We are not judged by some Almighty God, but our own higher dimensional aspect of being evaluates our own actions. Forgiveness comes from one's own self through a return to the realisation of the higher consciousness and recognition of Oneness. There is no eternal damnation for anyone, this is simply a notion created by Christianity in an attempt to control people by instilling fear into their hearts.

In this realm extra-terrestrial races have formed civilisations encompassing many star systems. The fifth dimension is usually the lowest dimension of being for the Star Beings. As the fifth dimension merges into the sixth (the Upper Astral), here is where we find a profusion of bizarre yet beautiful ethereal forms and beings. The highest reaches of the astral planes are comprised of very fine highly charged energetic vibrations and are populated by beings that can handle these vibrations. When we can heal ourselves deeply of energetic blockages, our chakra system is able to channel stronger spiritual energies into our being. We are then able to handle and perceive the powerful energies of the higher vibratory realities.

Huge matrices and honeycombs of rainbow light exist up here, hosting within them myriads of entities with rainbow bodies. These honeycombs are sixth dimensional shadows of almost inconceivable eighth and ninth di-

mensional structures. Contact with these honeycombs usually results in the transmission of information in the form of energy. If one is vibrationally attuned one can enter these honeycombs and even use them to travel beyond the astral into the galactic dimensions. Residents of the sixth dimension exist primarily as vibration and are experienced often as coloured current or waves to those on lower dimensions. They can transmit energy telepathically and energetically and appear to be part of huge matrices of intelligences. The full purpose of these beings is beyond current human comprehension.

In the sixth dimension, the notion of individuality changes into the notion of being part of the cosmos itself. One's consciousness can perceive multitudes of alien worlds at once, with time and space being transcended. It can seem as if one is looking at reality from another side. When the sixth dimensional energy is experienced temporarily by a third dimensional being one can see through everything, star systems and planets can be seen everywhere, along with huge rotating portal structures appearing in ones consciousness. Consciousness seems split in that one can no longer just see one thing. One can only see everything simultaneously. Many ideas and sensations can stream through the being, overloading the sensory system with large quantities of energy. Further bodily transmutation is then required to be able to assimilate and contain this level of vibration.

The energies can seem intense and overwhelming and it sometimes appears we may become lost into some limitless matrix. Familiarity with this dimension enables us to begin to realise that there is really nothing to fear. We have always been infinite, multidimensional beings, however the forgetting and the subsequent recollection of this reality gives rise to an initial fear. This requires transformation and releasing so the ascension process can continue.

It is important to remember that leaving the Earth for a higher dimension free from suffering and death is not possible until we have completed our karmic and personal obligations to the planet. Our part in the human situation must be fully healed and resolved before we will be able to reach a vibration high enough that we are able to ascend out of matter. Thus ascension is not a means of escaping the consequences of our actions. We must transform and heal our part in the planetary crisis before being able to leave.

Our physical bodies are ultimately an expression of unresolved karma. We are only on Earth with a body because we have lessons to learn and unresolved issues to heal here. When we do so, the underlying karmas that created our physical bodies are cleared, releasing us of bondage to three dimensional realities. I believe that approximately 10% of the human population will be able to transform all their karma and leave the Earth in 2012 and beyond and will ascend in light body form into the higher realms of existence.

As reality is relative depending on one's vibration it is possible for different individuals to have different views on reality. Each version will be a valid one and there is no absolute reality. Reality is determined by the vibratory level of the individual. So as we approach 2012, for those not consciously on a healing journey reality will remain fairly much the same, although unresolved issues will make life more challenging as the vibration of the Earth accelerates. For those not consciously wishing to heal and content as they are, the increase in the Earths vibration will bring anything unresolved to the fore and if several things surface at once then the individual will enter a period of intense healing crisis.

This surfacing of unresolved issues is unavoidable simply because the vibration of our bodies is increasing. Even if we are resistant to healing and change, the increased energies coming through at this current time will loosen some blockages in the system and force the healing. For people in this group, life will become very difficult unless they are able to become more receptive and open, surrender to the new consciousness attempting to flower within their being whilst developing a willingness to face and transform those aspects of themselves that are still unresolved.

For those individuals who have been on a healing path for many years and have embraced spiritual transformation, a remarkable ascension process will begin as higher dimensional energies are able to be assimilated into ones being without resistance. One can begin to have the experience of spiritual illumination and a lightness in body as outlined in the following extract from my internet blog;-

There will become a day in your life where if you have sincerely and deeply engaged with the spiritual path and undergone a healing journey you will begin to experience the Enlightenment.

The Enlightenment is a state of being where all the dualities, misconceptions, obscurities and sufferings collapse into the white light of the heart centre and all is seen and understood as it is. All things previously inaccessible or subconscious will rise into awareness. All your dreams will become lucid, rich, colourful, and full of meaning. Conscious astral travel will become the normality as you undertake nightly journeys to other-worldly dimensions of existence. Communing with the Star Beings there, you will be able to receive very detailed instructions and insights about how to live out the rest of your life on this dimension.

Every morning when you awaken, you will awaken into the awareness of the inner light and unbelievable amounts of energy will begin flowing through your chakra system. The kundalini current will draw all the chakras together into a unified operating energetic system as you transform into a fully integrated human being functioning optimally on all levels in preparation for the Ascension.

By this point you will feel such a deep current of Divinity flowing through you, that you will do nothing but surrender to the beautiful flow and unfolding of this higher consciousness. Every moment of your life you will be guided and abundance will flow from all directions.

All will be love, your heart will be pure and you will harbour no anger or resentment. All emotional sufferings will be completely healed and you will be able to stand strong and fearless in this time of great planetary change. You will feel deeply held and loved by the Universe and never will you not feel the love of the higher intelligences.

All your fears will finally give out, surrendering into the deeply heart expanding vibrations of higher consciousness. Nothing will remain of your fears, save for some memories of a past self wrapped up in fear and limited by ego. The transformation into the fearless loving spaces is so profound and so deeply rejuvenating to the heart and body that no words will fully describe these experiences.

The thing that will then become apparent is that most of the systems and structures created by humanity are dysfunctional and are not in accordance with higher dimensional wisdom. Answers to all manner of issues will become apparent where before there was a lack of understanding and insight. Realising this higher consciousness and integrating it into our current day systems is vital for the ascension and healing of humanity, if we are to avoid a chaotic collapse of human civilisation.

Now you will probably be able to see the inner light as well as feel it. The outer world will begin to radiate and the solidity begin to dissolve around you. Crown chakra activation will bring about the sensation of being able to rise out of physical reality and may be experienced as feeling your head has surfaced from a murky sea into some shiny sparkling divine matrix, along with an awareness of multidimensional consciousness manifesting as visions of alien worlds, angelic beings and other star systems. All this can be experienced whilst walking about in this dimension.

If you have done some healing work with your body it will become very light and you will notice the light vibrations transforming the physical body into higher form as the DNA blueprints for a new light body are activated.

This is the beginning of the ascension out of matter. The awareness of the inner light may become so strong and deep that it will feel like it is about to burst forth from your physical body. Sometimes your consciousness attention will shift to the light planes and you will see yourself as a luminous bundle of light hovering a metre or so off the ground and the physical body will not be visible.

This is a clear sign that you are entering into the crossover stage where the higher light energies are fully integrated into the heart and spirit in preparation for conscious Earth departure. It will be very apparent at this point that your life in this dimension is drawing to a close and that you will soon be able to ascend. This inner light will grow stronger and your vibration will accelerate to a degree where one day the physical body will no longer be able to contain such a high level of consciousness and it will fold back in upon itself, back into the light matrix from where it was created and you will be free. Free from body, you will become expansive and enlightened light consciousness. One day in the future, in one final outpouring of light you will finally depart from this realm, alive and conscious , never to take rebirth here again.

The invitation now for humanity is to collectively engage with our unresolved issues and by doing so, we are able to raise our consciousness and develop a deeper sensitivity of heart that will awaken us to the reality of our situation. Ultimately it is our karma and our fear that keeps us closed to higher possibilities, however by recognising the healing power of love, we can let it into our lives without resistance so it can do its healing work.

The collective psyche of humanity is currently in a state of denial of the effects that our actions are having on the ecosystem as a whole. We are so afraid to face the possible repercussions that we have become closed and so have refused to acknowledge or face the issues that threaten our long term survival. Instead we attach ourselves to material comforts and the economic philosophy that if we continue to expand the economy, business solutions will be found to fix our problems. The reality of the situation is that we actually have to totally renounce the current economic model, if we are to have any hope of making serious progress at healing the planet and saving our species from a large scale environmental and humanitarian disaster.

The challenge for humanity now is to move out of denial and to actually confront the deep fear that has gripped us and blinded us to the higher consciousness. This fear has kept us closed to the possibility of loving higher intelligences and in fact anything that presents itself as being a solution to our current predicament. It is the healing of fear, both on a collective and individual level now that is so crucial for humanity. By transforming fear we are able to stand strong and compassionate in the face of intense global change and upheaval.

Chapter 4

Healing
the fear

Fear and the ego are very closely connected to one another and can be likened to being two sides of the same coin – transcend one and you transcend the other. The ego can be seen as a very small part of our true nature although the ego wrongly seems to believe it is the whole of our nature. When the ego is presented with a different reality outside of its normal range or is challenged in some way that threatens its illusory sense of reality and domination, it has the tendency to react and thus we experience fear.

Fear in a limited sense is useful for it keeps us safe on the physical level. The fear mechanism would have been essential to the survival of primitive man, enabling them to run from wild animals and challenge rivals. However the fear mechanism is now outdated and we are in a situation where we have a fear of letting go of fear!

Fear is ultimately responsible for a lot of the conflicts on the planet today as fear breeds separation from love, and causes hatred and misunderstandings. The collective psyche of humanity is paralysed by fear and denial of our current environmental situation. Afraid to face the issues, it is not possible to find solutions. It will be necessary for the heart of humanity to be healed of fear. This can be done by collectively opening up to the love from the higher dimensions.

The ascension process calls on us to move beyond what we currently believe. Hence at some point on the journey we will undoubtedly experience fear. Fear is a formidable obstacle to ascension for if we are not able to transcend it, we will remain as we are and our vibratory level will remain below the threshold for the awakening of the higher consciousness. Fear saps us of our power and vitality to an extent very few of us actually realize. Fear of the higher realities can exist on a very subtle, almost undetectable level as well as on a more obvious level. For as long as this is the case we will not be able to integrate properly any new reality and experience the healing that can bring.

The fears that require healing for us to make the ascension into a new consciousness are the fear of death, the fear of love, the fear of existing outside of or losing the body and a fear of Higher Intelligences. If we are afraid of death, we will have too much attachment to the physical body and may have a difficult time when the time comes to die. It is the fear of death that has led humanity to collectively over consume in this life in an attempt to mask the inner void and lack of deeper meaning to life. We experience this when we do not understand the truth of immortality and when our connection with the higher realms is severed.

When we have no fear of death, many things happen to us. Firstly we become less attached to everything in life, for we realise that all things are impermanent and pass away. We become less traumatised by the passing away of someone we are close to, begin to value life and live each day in full conscious, loving awareness, with the knowledge that the time here is limited. Being at peace with the idea of death enables us to face the reality of death and passing, rather than shying away or hiding from the reality of it. Being unafraid of death carries with it the possibility of spiritual illumination and conscious ascension into other realities beyond the physical.

As I mentioned earlier, any fear will rob one of vitality and inner power, sapping ones vibration and limiting ones ascension into higher consciousness.

The reward for healing the fear of death is that one is gifted with being able to see into the higher dimensions and the afterlife. Sealing off the energetic leakage stemming from the fear of death boosts ones vibration to a level where one can perceive and integrate into ones being realities beyond the physical plane. It is then possible to receive love and healing from higher dimensional beings.

When humanity as a whole is able to perceive spiritual realities, then we will be able to receive the loving guidance and communication from the higher intelligences that are on hand to help us through this period of global change. Free from fear, with open hearts, we allow ourselves to receive the unconditional love and assistance from the higher planes. These intelligences are not our saviours, for we must do a lot of our own healing and spiritual work before we can make the contact. By the time we are able to make the contact with the higher intelligences we will have transformed and healed so much within ourselves, that we then merit their assistance.

Along with the fear of death, we must also look at our fear of non-human entities or aliens. There is a lot of negative propaganda in the mainstream regarding alien intelligence that manifests in the form of horror books and films, where aliens from outer space come to feed on vulnerable humans. This is deeply harmful as this has bred a deeper collective fear of higher intelligence that closes us off from the possibility of relationship with them. The reality is that any being able to transcend the physical dimension would have had to transform much fear, karma and misunderstanding about the nature of reality. With that in mind, any higher intelligence would be by nature benevolent, loving and spiritually illuminated.

The truth of these loving intelligences is that they are very wise, ancient, immortal and compassionate in a way that we cannot fully comprehend as yet. We may find them to be undiscovered aspects of ourselves. If we are able to clear fear from our hearts, we open ourselves up to the possibility of a deeply loving and healing relationship with them. The culmination of healing my own fear resulted in a very profound contact experience with them, as described in an extract from my earlier writings;-

It is good never to underestimate the power of fear in keeping us separated from Divinity and from deeper relationship with the Universe. This experience came to me after 15 years of spiritual work, through meditation, body cleansing and self development. Though healing all of our fears seems a formidable obstacle, it is worth the perseverance, no matter how difficult the passage seems.

For fear and the ensuing erroneous perception of duality is the cause of every single suffering on this planet. Every war, every heartache, every tear shed is the manifestation of a suffering that is so unnecessary, stemming from a misconception of the way things are –if we can transform ourselves and remember all is love and surrender to the love, we will never have to experience any suffering again, for we accept everything as it is. In a space of total acceptance all is fine, just as it is. There is nothing to struggle for, to disagree with, to resist or to be afraid of. Healing all the fear acts as a conscious portal to high vibratory light realms.

I found myself in the luminous astral plane surrounded by the Star Beings, faces radiating incredible beauty, Divinity and pure love. I was on the shore of a distant world and the night sky was illuminated by many hundred blue stars. They encouraged me to look within my being and look for any fear. So I looked deep within my spirit, expecting to find some complex to work with or some fear standing in the way of a deeper experience of them. I then realised for the first time in my life that actually there was no fear alighting anywhere in my being. All was peaceful, the heart was still and I saw every fear I had held onto float away on the waters of this distant shore. I bade farewell to my old self, across the waters of this beautiful planet - an old self so limiting and no longer serving. Finally fear had disentangled itself from the core spiritual vibration of my being, setting me free.

This aspect of myself never resisted the parting, finally letting go, realising that never again could it hold any power over me. As a searing bliss rose within, the departing fear dissolved and went its own way back into the vibrations of the cosmos. The ego had realised its false nature and far across the waters I saw something rise and enter into the celestial skies.

Tall luminous crystalline towers stretched to incredible altitudes, an outward symbol of a civilisation with very advanced technological abilities. The buildings themselves seemed to be conduits for higher dimensional energies and just looking at them resulted in the experience of feeling energy surges and a strange familiarity. To enter one of these towers would enable one to leave the galaxy and travel several billion light years across physical space in almost an instant. I understood that these portals led one into regions of hyperspace where the Divine Caretakers of the Universe exist – those intelligences that can create galaxies and stars simply through thought. I can feel their vibrations radiating out of the tower, and light rays enter my heart. There are no words that can communicate this kind of love. One just has to experience it for oneself to understand. When humanity realises this level of love and intelligence, we will realise our true nature and the level of healing that will come about on Earth will be nothing short of total.

Then the beings came closer. They communicated that the final passage of moving out of fear had been completed and never again would I be separated from them and every day of my life, I will stand strong and fearless on the Earth, so as to be an instrument for the healing of others. Then a glorious white star rose above the waters and out of it emerged these hyper-conscious intelligences, winged beings, encrusted with the jewels of the light vibrations, multicoloured, glowing and deeply loving. I felt so held and unconditionally loved by these beings. They said that fear had kept myself and others from sharing such a deep relationship with them. With no fear, we can enter into relationship with them, a sharing so deeply loving, profound and enriching that any Earthly relationship pales in comparison. In this deep relationship with the Higher Beings all is open, nothing is held *back and there is always an abundance of love. The more we are able to open to them, the more healing we can receive.*

Then I saw bundles of old karmas depart from my being and they were cast into the fires of the Great Central Sun, absolved and annihilated through recognition of inner luminosity. From myriads of stars emerged a whole array of deeply loving intelligences to witness this transition. They opened portals into higher dimensional hyperspace and gave me a hyper-energetic vibrational key which fitted into my auric matrix so as to enable transdimensional astral travel. There was the vision of majestic, smooth, shiny pyramids floating in the depths of space, and closer examination revealed infinitely intricate alien markings and inscriptions which then just burst apart into light. There were these cubic space craft which opened to reveal incredibly luminous light orbs. World after world appeared, alien yet beautiful, appearing as huge shimmering hyper-globes, surface manifestations of a much deeper dimensional reality as yet inconceivable. These alien worlds contained orbital spinning structures, highly technological buildings, domes and crafts fully decked out with luminous and pulsating panels, as well as portals into other finer vibrational realities.

Then I popped into some new realm, a realm of bubbles in a translucent liquid. The Star Beings said;-

"Look, there is your universe, your reality, your vibration – as they showed me one tiny bubble amongst a backdrop of millions more. This dimension is where universes are birthed and where they collapse back into at the end of their cycle. In this vibration you are immune

to the death of a planet or the supernova of a star. Here you are so far outside of time that you are nothing other than immortal singularity – you are the Universe and so much more. When you fully integrate this reality into your home dimension, you will be able to be in several places at once and walk through matter. You will be able to heal everything on your planet and see into the deepest reaches of space simply through the medium of your own consciousness."

"You will discover technologies that will take you to Alpha Centauri in minutes and to another Galaxy in less than a day of your time. Harnessing the energy from the higher dimensions, your energy crisis on Earth will be over and no one on your planet will ever be in need of anything. Famines, wars, environmental disasters, oil spills, they will all be a thing of the past. Nuclear waste will be easily removable from your planet along with your nuclear arsenals and an era of peace and enlightenment will come to your world that will lift you from the brink of earthly extinction to a place amongst the stars. A vibration of love, so pure, powerful and transformative is set to enter every single unilluminated corner of human existence and everything will be transformed. All of your suffering and lacking on Earth has arisen from failing to recognise your connection to the Source, which provides you with infinite intelligence, love and abundance."

"Suffering is not a necessary part of existence. All your misfortunes, sicknesses and sorrows are all manifestations of a being that is not energetically connected to the Higher Vibrations. In our worlds, there is no death or illness, nor is there ever lacking or unfulfilled need. All is infinite here and we are pure essence vibration – you

are too, although it is difficult for you to realise it whilst encapsulated in the density of a karmic body. But you can heal so you do not have to have a body anymore and then you are free of all the associated sufferings."

"Now the universe is yours to explore, go where you will, visit the stars, know us deeply and never be separated from us again. Your incarnation into the lower vibrations of fear and illusion separated you from us. We always loved you and we waited for you to make this journey back to these vibrations. The doors to the higher realms are now open for you."

The teachings from these incredibly evolved intelligences communicate that the human condition can be transcended simply through a resolution of karma. Final resolution of karma brings about the birthing of hyperspace consciousness in humanity, with the ensuing realisation that the Earth plane is a very limiting reality.

We can also achieve a far more favourable karmic outcome through resolving our fears and issues. With a full luminous awareness, we can see any outward manifestation of difficulty or suffering is a reflection of something within ourselves in need of healing. When we are fully aware of our whole being, we heal blockages before they cause disruption in our lives, thus misfortune through hidden cause is eliminated and nothing can catch us unaware.

The Star Beings carry such deep love, that contact will open our hearts on the deepest level so that all defilements and impurities can be resolved and healed. We can then feel the full magnitude and beauty of the love these beings have for us. In that place we are held, guided, and nurtured all the way to our final liberation. All it requires is surrender within ourselves so that we may be open to the highest healings and open to receiving from these higher intelligences. We can then finally depart from this sphere of suffering and illusion, where we have lingered for far too long.

So to heal our fear, we first need to find it and to do this we must look deeper into our being, and we will find our deepest fears lurking as a quiet, dense, energetic shadow almost exactly superimposed upon ourselves. This subtler, hidden aspect of fear is what takes our energy and prevents us from reaching our true potential. It will be the root cause of doubt, lack of confidence and a whole other range of negative emotions, as well as unhelpful thought patterns that no longer serve us.

This subtle fear is closely bound to the ego-self in such a way it is almost indistinguishable without deep self-enquiry. When we see it for what it is, it then dissolves as it is illusory and has no substantial nature. Rather it is simply a complex of limiting, false and unhelpful thought patterns bundled up in a package masquerading as a real self. We then falsely identify with that as our real self and thus we feed the illusion. It then grows, draws energy round itself and condenses, cloaking our multidimensional light body with dark energy, keeping us imprisoned to the physical plane and in a three dimensional body. We are then separated from the higher realities.

When we are able to see through the illusion of the ego-self and when any fear subsides, we will find ourselves in an infinitely loving, divine, expansive and vibrant space. This is the realm of the spirit, of the higher dimensional planes, a higher and truer reality that always exists within us, but is obscured by the obfuscations and fabrications of the ego mind. This is the main part of our spiritual journey, to ascend out of the quagmire of the ego-fed realities into the shining radiance of the higher planes.

So how can we deal with the ego and this subtle lurking fear? We must go to the edges of our comfort zones within our consciousness through whatever means we choose (meditation, shamanic work or counselling) – and go where the furthest reaches of ego meet the vibrations of the higher dimensions. There we will come face to face with our shadow - the false self that believes itself real. Here we must abide a while, for at the edges of our comfort zones we are often close to the healing higher dimensional vibrations. When the ego self is exposed to the higher vibrations transformation can occur. It can be incredibly intense and we may be tempted to shy back from these realms. But if we remain, the denser parts of our ego begin to dissolve into the light and our overall vibration is cleansed. We are empowered and invigorated with the vibration of truth. We see how the ego is nothing more than a construct of the mind, a fortress built by itself to self perpetuate itself. For many never realise the illusory nature of this construct or even that it exists, but it is there.

In these higher dimensional spaces we can examine closely this sense of ego, of self, to find out exactly where it is. The more we enquire, the more we find this ego self is a shimmering facade that has no residence anywhere in the body or mind and the notion of it can be seen to be surrounded by the vibrations of the infinite. At some point on our journey we will realise that the infinite actually pervades the entire self, rather than just surrounding it. In these moments of great fear we may hold on intensely to our sense of self and if we then have enough courage to continue the enquiry we will simply realise the infinite is everywhere and there is simply no self anywhere to be found. There are only the vibrations of the Divine. Love, peace, expansiveness and freedom are everywhere and it is as if we have emerged from a stiff, constraining cocoon as a butterfly with newly formed wings. Free from ego and fear we can now explore these realms of love and light.

The longer that we can consciously spend in the borderlands where ego meets the infinite, the more fear that can be dissolved as the fortress walls begin to crumble. Energetically we become lighter as fear dissolves into empowerment and love, insight and enlightening visions. As we identify more with the higher realms, we begin to lose our fears, our shadow begins to lose its power over us and our energy increases. With fear well behind us on our path we can achieve much and transform our lives beyond recognition.

So how can we speed up this process? We have to find our hidden fears, face them and bring them out into the light, whilst being gentle and loving to ourselves for it can sometimes be a difficult and harrowing journey. However the end rewards are high and ultimately the survival of humanity is dependent on many of us completing this healing work. The ego thrives on what no longer serves us, so we would do well to develop a deeper awareness of all the old energies and attachments we are carrying around in our vibration.

Anything that no longer serves us creates a stagnation and density in our aura that weighs down on and cloaks our light bodies. As we let these things go, whether they be fears, unhelpful habits, unnecessary possessions or outgrown relationships, our vibration becomes lighter and finer. The less we carry in our vibration, the lighter and happier our journey will be.

Fear ultimately is healed by love. By learning to trust love and inviting it into our hearts we open and in that opening the fear can begin to dissolve. Fear and love cannot exist simultaneously. When we are in a space of love, there is no fear. The invitation now for us, collectively and individually, is to master the ability to stay in the heart space and operate from there at all times.

Humanity today is suffering from a deficiency of love, which has bred fear, separation, distrust and conflict. The heart of humanity is deeply wounded, but can be healed through coming together for the common good whilst developing an open attitude toward healing and spiritual development. By identifying the causes of suffering and how we have descended into fear, we can begin the transformation and begin to find a collective unity which can go a long way to healing conflict. Healing conflicts on a regional level also heals the heart of humanity on a global level. With this is mind, the individual also has a part to play. For if we are not in our own hearts and in a space of love, how can we expect to see global peace and harmony?

If global peace and harmony is what we desire, we have to start with ourselves and begin the healing. Whatever stands in the way of us becoming more loving beings needs resolution and more often than not, the underlying root cause will be fear and an attachment to the ego-self. The ego creates a fictitious reality and then projects it outwards, the subsequent identification with this reality creates all the suffering known to humanity. As it is a fictitious projection and not based on the true reality of Light and Love, then suffering is perpetuated and exacerbated as we are not operating from open, fearless and loving spaces.

If we are able to project a false reality onto the outer world and not recognise it, then we can also fall into the trap of projecting all kinds of negative aspects of ourselves that we are unwilling to acknowledge outwardly. We then develop the false belief that these qualities exist outside of ourselves and are not part of our own inner make up. This trap prevents us from healing on a very deep level by preventing us developing a full awareness of our wounded true self. Recognising the ego-self and its ability to project can heal our being of almost everything, but it requires one to face the undiluted and almost overwhelming fear of moving beyond the comfort zones and the false sense of security created by the ego. There are many ways of doing this; through meditation or breath work, psychedelic or shamanic exploration, dream work, near death experience or through exposure to ego shattering or heartbreaking experiences in life that force us to see the larger picture and see beyond ourselves.

When this spiritual work is practised for long enough, there will be a day where one identifies more with the Divine, non-dual, loving, spiritual core essence of being, rather than the illusory ego self. When that occurs the ego will be seen as a total illusion along with all the associated realities it has created. It will then be seen that suffering too is an illusion, a fabrication, an imagined reality and though appearing very real and unavoidable for many of us, a doorway exists for all of us through which we can walk out of suffering at any time through letting go of the attachment to ego.

It should not be underestimated how powerful attachment to ego is in creating and causing all of the conditions necessary for human suffering. If through fear we have created the illusion of ego, we will need to either deconstruct it through recognising love and healing the fear or continue to feed the illusion. The latter can only be done by spinning and maintaining an elaborate web of control games and programmed responses based on fiction that keep the illusion going. Anything that then challenges the reality of the ego, or its protective programming, is seen as a threat and thus any situation or being that appears on our path carrying a higher truth or an invitation to surrender to a more loving reality will bring up deep fear, which can only be healed by moving into the heart and seeing beyond the self.

Only through the painful, albeit necessary deconstructing and dismantling of the programming created by the ego, will we be able to find lasting peace, spiritual illumination and a way out of suffering. This dismantling of the fortress walls can be undergone voluntarily through having a willingness to look at ourselves in a new light and beginning the transformative work. If we are resistant, then often the Universe will bring forth situations that will cause us a lot of pain and suffering until we realise the futility of holding on to outdated, outgrown and erroneous beliefs.

When we begin this work, we will have to go through many 'passages' in which we may feel like we are dying or totally devoid of love, or we may feel cast aside on some spiritual wasteland, withering and dying, in the fire of suffering, praying for some Divine deliverance to bring us out of this self created illusion. It is through these passages of ego dissolution that we are faced with the illusion, called to see through it and become aware of higher consciousness. In these difficult passages, we are humbled to our core and at the time it may feel like we are broken, however this is only another illusion of the ego and in retrospect we are thankful for the experience. We are then spiritually reborn into a new reality where ego is permanently weakened and higher spiritual realities are incorporated into our belief structures.

The more of these passages we can endure, the higher is our level of healing and ultimately this process has the potential to bring about a full enlightenment and a total freedom from suffering. We may still have to sometimes experience what other people may see as suffering, but we see it simply as experience with no negative or aversive attributes attached to it. When suffering is totally accepted as it is, it ceases to be suffering and the karmic cycle is broken, the ego programming is destroyed and the higher realities begin to shine forth.

When we are standing in a space of pure love and light, suffering or difficult experiences simply do not come to us and we can receive deep guidance and protection from things or situations that would otherwise harm us. There are accounts of people who when faced with a charging lion or tiger have held their composure, standing in fearlessness and radiating love, as a result the animal has either turned away and disappeared or simply become calm and lay down, no longer a threat.

When we are healed of fear, we can begin the work of the transformation of our collective consciousness through love. It is love, above anything else that can do the most healing work in humanity. When we love, we accept others unconditionally and wholeheartedly, we are open to sharing, we come together with common purpose with the ability to listen, communicate and embrace truth. It is these attributes that will become deeply valuable in the healing of humanity and the restoration of our planet. At the same time, we will not be afraid to stand fearless, firm but in a loving way, to offer peaceful resistance to those intent on destroying our planet, perpetuating the fears and causing more conflicts. When they see more of us refusing to bow down to this manifestation of fear and darkness, then it makes it far more likely that more of these misguided individuals and groups will relinquish their attachments to ego and fear, returning to the space of love and beginning their healing.

The biggest danger humanity faces now is from those that do not wish to surrender their fears and wish to prevent other people from healing and integrating the higher consciousness. For some they simply do not know how; others have malevolent intent. Toward this group of people we should have compassion, for it is this segment of humanity that stands to suffer the most as the rest of humanity finds a deeper healing. Not everybody is able to embrace the new consciousness. For some the only karmic resolution for them will be a difficult death out of this world, created by their own unwillingness to let go of the old stories, the fear, and the agendas of aggression and domination.

We will come to value these individuals as spiritual teachers, for they will show the clear options available to those that still have time to choose their own destiny - enlightenment and liberation from suffering, or the intense suffering of death and destruction. Humanity often fears 'end of the world' scenarios, however this is not something inflicted on us at random. We are the masters of our own destiny, we carry within us the potential for both destruction and liberation, and the ultimate outcome is down to the choices that each and every one of us makes. Unchecked and unaddressed fear stands to do much damage to humanity and our planet, but at the same time healing fear and embracing love carries far more power and the transformative ability to bring about much needed change. So much so that even at what is surely the eleventh hour for humanity, many can still be healed, much suffering can still be avoided, and the outcome can still be a positive one for the collective as a whole.

Chapter 5

Seeing through
the illusion

When we fully awaken to our Star seed consciousness, having dispensed with fear and embraced love, it will very quickly become manifest that most of the ego-based consciousness is a total fabrication – a shimmering facade – and an illusion. The type of consciousness that exists beyond the ego is based on pure love and light. Centred in the heart one can see through all the workings and dynamics of ego.

It will become apparent that most individuals within humanity are wearing 'masks' and are pretending to be a self that they are not. As many of us are wounded in some way, we are afraid to acknowledge and face those true aspects of ourselves. Instead we invest our energies in the creation of a false self and reality that brings a sense of temporary comfort and an escape from seeing our true self, but prevents us from reaching a space of enlightenment and liberation from fear and suffering. For the false self is created upon a sense of fear and it cannot allow itself to be loved or healed, for to do so would require the admission of the false self that it is living a lie. To acknowledge this would call for the underlying wounded self to be seen and the painful healing process to begin. Hence for some people it is more comfortable to remain living in the lie.

Thus for those living a life wearing the mask of false self, there is a continuing story of suffering and a lack of love, and because so many are living this life, this has contributed to the collective heart of humanity becoming separated from love and unable to face the issues that need resolution for us to reach a higher level of consciousness. Often the origin of this false self comes from a fear space, which often is a sign of a wounded inner child. When we have the strength and courage to face and heal our inner child, with a loving and gentle awareness, we have the potential to become free from our deepest fears, to become strong in vibration and pure in heart.

Having completed those healings, we will have no reason to continue to perpetuate the illusion of false self, and can instead identify with the true self. As the true self by this point has been healed, there is capacity for deep love and wisdom. It is this loving wisdom that can then see through the distortions and lies created by the projections of the false self. We will also then be able to see through a wide array of power game dynamics that are at play between most individuals and groups within humanity and are the cause of every kind of conflict imaginable.

Being able to see through these dynamics is very transformative for ourselves and others we come into contact with, for if we are fully in the Light and living from a place of truth and love, it will not be possible for us to be covertly manipulated or controlled by any kind of harmful energy dynamic. Thus the person wearing the mask will either need to take the power game elsewhere or to surrender and take off the mask, give up the attachment to a false reality and show themselves as they really are by revealing their vulnerabilities and hurts. In this space they have the potential to receive the love they need and to begin a deep and thorough healing process. Fully healed beings do not need to engage in energy games, being energetically whole and connected to Source.

These power game dynamics that are very prevalent in humanity are basically control games that are played often subconsciously and thus outside of awareness, to maintain the illusion of ego self, to replay old control dramas and to obtain psychic energy from other human beings. A being separated from the Source will be consistently deficient in spiritual nourishment and will erroneously believe that the only way to compensate for that is to compete with others to draw it from them. This works for a time, but spiritual evolution and growth always presides in the end and some kind of intense suffering such as the end of an unhealthy relationship, will bring awareness to the inner wounds and the energy dynamics at work and present an opportunity for healing. It is possible to avoid this intense suffering through consciously working with ourselves at the earliest opportunity and getting in touch with the heart to find those wounds in need of healing.

For as long as we engage in these power games, we will never attain a lasting sense of happiness or reach a higher state of healing and enlightenment. Healing comes from finding our connection to the Source and becoming a whole human being, which then raises our consciousness above the need for suffering. Engagement in power games is always draining, for we will never draw to us sufficient energy and the sense of completeness we seek. We also perpetuate the reality of fear, incompleteness and inner lack, which draws to us endless rounds of pain and suffering until we recognise the deeper fears and wounded parts of ourselves that prevent us from living a reality of love and freedom from suffering.

For those that attempt to control others through covert manipulation and power struggles, the root cause of this behaviour is a state of deep unresolved fear. If we have a need to control another human being, it is invariably because they represent an aspect of ourselves we are not willing to face and so by controlling the other we seek to repress or deny these aspects of ourselves and attempt to maintain a sense of "status quo". As strong and powerful as this position appears to be, and in the world today we see it maintained by brutality, murder, suppression and brute force - it is ultimately a weak and vulnerable position because it is fear based. In the face of love and light, these control dynamics will become weak, powerless and meaningless when seen for what they are. Love is inherently powerful and always presides in the end.

However the power of love is only used or exerted upon others for their benefit. This power is of a much greater magnitude than the illusion of power currently being perpetuated by the global status-quo and as such only those with a discernment and moral purity will be able to use it, and which only comes after a long period of deep holistic purification of all negativities and toxic accumulations in the body. When we move away from fear into love, we will be bestowed with this immense clarity and power, it is this purer state of being that will have the ability to heal the world once the agendas of the fear based ruling elite fall apart.

As well as those who control, there are those who allow themselves to be controlled and this is because they have ineffective or non-existent boundaries. This too is a manifestation of emotional wounds and stems from a lack of self love and broken self-esteem. In this place we allow others to manipulate and control us and then play victim when it happens, making them out to be solely responsible. This is the other aspect of the power game dynamic which is equally as harmful - allowing oneself to be controlled by it. By healing our own self worth issues, repairing our own self-esteem, addressing our fears and expressing clear boundaries with loving communication, we become energetically whole and restored and thus immune to any kind of manipulation or control.

These dynamics are most evident in human intimate relationships where all the wounded aspects of ourselves come forth calling for resolution. It is in this area where the greatest opportunities for healing these deeper wounds exist. Often we will be drawn to those who reflect back to ourselves our wounded aspects and the ensuing conflict so widespread in romantic relationships begins when we refuse to see ourselves as the cause of our suffering, and project it out onto the other. Only after a lot of heartache and suffering do we finally develop the awareness and desire to heal the wounds. Then our relationships become far more harmonious and fluidic. Unbound by projection they are free to find more spiritual ways of expression and become opportunities to move deeper into the heart. Healing the heart of humanity thus calls for each of us to engage with our own relationship healing and to resolve those issues that draw us into conflict with others. When our heart is deeply healed, conflict becomes rare in our lives and we experience wellbeing and deep harmonious interactions with other people.

Another dynamic in human interactions that causes a lot of suffering and requires healing is what I call the Saviour complex. This is a situation where someone falls in love with another person and then believes they can save them from all suffering and fix all their problems. Though appearing altruistic at first, on a deeper level the driving force behind this behaviour is to recreate old traumas in the heart of the 'saviour'. It is ultimately an outward indication of someone lacking validation in early life and by being drawn to someone with deep wounds, they will be unable to receive the love and validation they seek, and thus the trauma is re-experienced. Invariably the 'rescued' sees the 'saviour' as the cause of their pain for it is too painful for them to confront it in themselves. So they then strike out at the 'saviour' in unloving ways making him or her feel invalidated. This then invites the 'saviour' to find validation and love from within which then heals the complex and avoids the necessity of later conflict in future relationships.

It is important for us to have compassion for other suffering people, but at the same time we all have a responsibility for our own issues and as spiritual beings we need to develop a discernment between helping someone who is in genuine need and helping someone who does not wish to step out of their old control dramas. Some people will need to go deeper into their illusions and suffering before they are able to be helped.

Healing our relationships is a vital part of healing ourselves fully on the emotional level which assists in raising our consciousness out of suffering. Unresolved emotional issues perpetuate all kinds of suffering so

prevalent on the planet today; family breakdowns, relationship failures, violence, alcoholism, and crime - to
name just a few. Unresolved emotional issues will ultimately cause disease and death if not addressed. The
greatest healing and inner empowerment comes from
healing our inner child and conversely, not doing so
ultimately leads to our demise. When we are at peace
with our inner child we are often freed from all fear and
relinquish the need to control others, we are then able to
love others with an open and tender heart.

Those who control us can only do so if we are carrying
some kind of fear it can hook onto. Our inner fears feed
the power dynamic and so by healing the fears, we heal
not only our part in it but the controlling person's part
too, for they are made more aware of the dynamic when
their fuel supply (collective or individual fear) runs out.
They are then called to begin their journey to wholeness
and spiritual healing.

So, looking at the global situation today, we see a lot of
suppression and control by the dominating elite with
dubious agendas. The elite, along with a compliment of
very rich companies with extensive business portfolios
apparently in control of the world, appear to be in a very
powerful position. However this is illusory and ultimately their position is weak for it is not underpinned by
love or ethical values and their main construction - the
global economy, has been in serious trouble for some
time. I believe this is evidence of more of us seeing
through the illusions created by fear and so the system is
beginning to crumble and lose its power over the common people.

The world economy is currently based on fiction and an erroneous sense of reality, in that it perpetuates the belief in a sense of lack or need and that the answers to those deficiencies are to consume ever more to find happiness and satisfaction. The true reality is that the Universe is infinitely abundant in energy and love and when we come back to our spiritual centre and become whole, we receive all the nourishment we need from the higher spiritual planes.

There can be a tendency for us to see ourselves as the victim, at the mercy of these powerful corporations and political structures that are doing immense environmental and societal damage to humanity and the planet. Our healing here is to move past the victim consciousness, and to realise we have fed these structures with our collective fears.

We have given our power to them and disempowered ourselves in the process by allowing them to dominate and control us. When we restore our hearts to a state of perfect love, the healthy boundaries will be reinstated, we will see through the lies and fabrications that they are perpetuating and their power and control over us will diminish. As the outer world always reflects our inner state of healing, we can then expect to see the formation of love based economies and political structures that have the spiritual and emotional wellbeing of humanity at heart. It will be these new structures founded upon love that will bring an end to global inequality, hunger and a lot of the unnecessary suffering associated with globalization and excessive economic development.

As we heal our own fears, the old structures still holding to fear will have to give way and collapse. When we heal our own self-worth and find an inner abundance, the world banking system built on debt will also collapse. The ensuing chaos may seem extreme for a time, but the important thing is to hold to the Light and remain in a space of love and trust that this is a global healing process that needs to happen. It is possible to become immune to any suffering in this collapse by healing all of one's fears and karmas prior to the event and by raising ones level of consciousness as high as possible through bodily and emotional healing. The elite, as they disband and begin to lose their power may well panic and attempt to throw people in prison, or threaten people with draconian laws in an attempt to quell the uprising. This will be ineffective, for by this point so many people will have awakened, that the power of love will have become an unstoppable force of healing and the only option left for the old elite is to surrender, let go of their agendas, and begin their healing, if they are to avoid a difficult passage out of this dimension.

If we wish to bring about a new world of global harmony and peace, it is vital to refrain from any kind of violent protest, or even having thoughts of hatred toward the corporations. For this too strengthens their position and does nothing to heal ones underlying fear. It is only humility and love that have the power to bring about deep and profound changes on this planet. As the world transitions and the old structures collapse, it is inevitable that there will be a significant rise in the number of human deaths. Rather than retreating from the fact in fear, it is more valuable to realise that this too is all part of the healing as humanity gives back to nature and decreases in size to a more sustainable level.

For some people, the only way to clear karma and raise their consciousness is through death and as we are entering a period of intense karmic healing, then we will naturally see more death. For these people, incorporating the higher dimensional energies into their bodies is beyond them- and for those unable to heal deep issues, death offers resolution. When the fear of death is healed and the bigger spiritual picture is seen, none of this is frightening or disturbing. Rather it is seen simply as a healing process. Those who choose to leave through death at this time are also teaching those that remain behind the value of compassion in the face of human suffering. Compassion opens the heart, develops a deeper sensitivity and eliminates fear. For those who die in the transitions, provided they have lived well they will journey to the higher ascended planes and meet the Star Beings in spirit form. They will receive guidance, love and assistance with their individual paths to ascension.

For those who have been intent on spreading fear, impeding the progress of humanity and being responsible for large scale exploitation, poisoning, environmental destruction and the maintaining of fear based oppressive regimes, there will be no way to avoid the karmic consequences of those actions. For these individuals and groups there lies a very difficult spiritual passage ahead where all those aspects of oneself that one has refused to heal or transform will be presented in the form of extremely intense suffering, for which there will be little alleviation. These individuals involved in the dark agendas and perpetuating fear will become overwhelmed with their own fears and are liable to become very ill. As their bodies begin to break down from the toxic effects of their own creations, no amount of medical assistance will be able to save these people from a difficult death as the cause will be of a much deeper, karmic, spiritual nature.

In deep fear, weakened and dying, these people who once were part of empires that fed on the suffering of others and sought to control and dominate everything that lives and breathes on this planet, will become totally disempowered and will have to endure a very difficult passage out of this world. They will find themselves reincarnated on other lower dimensional worlds, products of their own karmas and will have to experience many lifetimes of extreme suffering until their karmas are resolved. Their reign of domination on Earth will be over with their departure from the Earth plane, for the increase in the vibration of the Earth will make rebirth here for these groups impossible.

However long after their departure, the shells of their physical empires on Earth will remain. The abandoned skyscrapers built by the multi-billion dollar banking industry will stand empty as the new humanity rebuilds a civilization in the surrounding areas. It is likely that the new humanity will leave these structures standing, as a massive open air museum and a reminder to all that the efforts of those who thought they could globalize the planet and control everything ultimately came to nothing. Within a few decades, nature will take back these structures, vines, creepers and trees will eventually weaken the foundations and these empty towers will come crashing to the ground soon after 2100. By this point, most of the economic cities of the world will simply be decaying carcasses of the Old World Order as the new humanity will not choose to live in this way, in a gross violation of the laws of nature. It is likely that at this point, many humans will be living in small green settlements and will also have at their disposal a wide range of green advanced technologies. Whilst living harmoniously on the Earth, they will be able to visit the stars with ease and will enjoy open contact with the Star Beings.

As we progress with our spiritual healing, the extent of the illusion becomes apparent and we see that almost the entirety of our human lives have been built around the belief in a fixed self and a material world without any spiritual counterpart. Spiritual enlightenment comes about after a long period of deep reflection and the questioning of everything we have been brought up to believe. The truths that are suppressed and hidden from us, human origins, ET contact, ruined alien cities on Mars as well as the truths behind all of the economic and political scandals on the planet, are the ones we need to discover and understand so as to facilitate our ascension out of this fictitious reality, which is nothing other than an outward projection created by an illusory ego-self. At some point, we then realise that all of the structures of the three dimensional world are designed to keep us enslaved to it and to prevent us seeing beyond it. The whole three dimensional world has been built to perpetuate the illusions of lack, energy scarcity, the absence of spirituality and that this life is all there is.

When we finally raise our consciousness high enough to see through the illusions, we will be rewarded with a new version of reality, richer, deeper and far more beautiful than the one we have believed in for so long. A reality of immortality, infinite love and an awareness of cosmic consciousness await us, bringing the possibility of contact with the Higher Beings. The ego is seen for what it is - a fabrication, and we then identify with the spiritual essence of our being instead, bringing about liberation, deep healing and deliverance from suffering. We will then be able to see through any lie or illusion presented to us by any corporation, government, or individual human being. It will be possible to see the agendas of any being not in accordance with the Light and in this space nothing can possibly harm us, we become immune to harm from the Dark Forces (those intent on perpetuating fear and hatred) and become stronger channels of pure love and light.

Chapter 6

Toxicity and vibratory purification

Humanity is currently overrun with toxicity on all levels, causing all manner of problems from physical diseases and broken hearts to poisoned eco-systems and raging conflicts with no end in sight. If we are to receive deep healing and become spiritually purified, then all of the toxins in our systems need to be identified and eliminated. At the same time, the current state of ignorance and denial that is prevalent around many of these toxins needs to be addressed also. In many of my encounters with the Star Beings, they emphasise how they are free from all suffering and disease and that the vibration of humanity is contaminated with all kinds of impurities that keep our hearts closed and overcome with fear, whilst keeping our bodies in a state of disease. As a result our spiritual faculties function at low levels, if at all.

Disease is not a necessary condition for any individual to experience. Diseases are not random afflictions that we have to endure, but instead they are outward expressions of an unhealed underlying root cause. Healing any disease properly, rather than simply alleviating the symptoms and making it appear the disease has gone away, is about identifying and addressing the underlying cause. The root cause of any illness or suffering will either be physical toxicity, inadequate nutrition or unresolved emotional issues and traumas. Purification and healing will need to occur on all levels if we are to become free from sickness and disease.

The physical body is a good starting point for healing, for though our ultimate destination may be in realms where we do not require a body, if we are to reach those realms, the body being the vehicle for the higher consciousness needs to be in optimum condition and free from toxins. When our physical body, notably the heart is free of toxicity - we can then develop a deeper degree of emotional sensitivity which facilitates emotional healing. If our physical hearts are clogged with toxins by eating the wrong kinds of foods or by exposure to other toxins, then it will not be possible for our emotional centre to be fully operational and clear of blockages. Thus the physical and emotional levels are intimately interlinked and the proper healing of one cannot occur without looking at the other. Hence the treating of disease purely by looking at the physical body prevalent in many of the medical institutions, does not bring about a deeper healing, for often there will be an emotional aspect to the disease.

We cannot look to the conventional medical systems to offer us any kind of lasting healing for many of their treatments create more problems than they treat. Although there have been some notable medical advances over the years, there has also been a ridiculously large number of deaths through prescription drugs, which is now a high ranking cause of death in the United States. Many of these prescribed drugs treat one symptom but cause numerous other side effects which often require further drugs, to the point where some people in care and nursing homes are on ten or so different medications on a daily basis to keep them alive and to manage side effects from all of these drugs.

At the same time, large numbers of the population die each year from cancer, heart disease and diabetes. There has been little reduction in the occurrences of these diseases and though many drugs have been created to increase longevity in patients, little effort has been made at identifying the causes of disease. When likely causes are suggested they are either ignored or suppressed. There exist numerous natural remedies for cancer, however when these are promoted they are quickly suppressed, and the person who discovered the treatment is often harassed by the authorities and sometimes they disappear or die in what appears to be an accident. I will leave it to the reader to draw their own conclusions from this.

The prevention of these diseases lies in proper nutrition and a body free from internal toxicity. Much effort is spent today promoting beauty products and the like so we appear clean and pure on the outside, but there is little thought to the internal state of affairs. Many doctors today for example, do not recognize colonic irrigation (bowel cleansing) as being a valuable alternative treatment. If we wish to raise our bodily vibration and bring about healing, a good starting place is the bowel. It is our main organ of elimination, and needs to be in optimum condition. If we do not evacuate the bowel often enough, eat the wrong foods, or the bowel walls become clogged with old material, then this will prevent the bowel absorbing nutrients, which is another of its vital functions.

I can testify that after a series of colonic treatments, an improvement in bodily health and mental clarity was marked. However when one moves on to an appropriate cleansing diet, the need for colonics falls away as a proper diet with plenty of raw vegetables provides all the nutrition and materials necessary to keep the bowel clean and in optimum condition. When the bowel is in a poor state of health and is sluggish, then emotional toxins will also accumulate and lead to poor emotional wellbeing, and can lead to outbreaks of aggression, anger and even violence.

Before I discuss emotional detoxification in more depth, there are some other physical toxins worth discussing as well as the appropriate diet for raising our vibration. With regard to physical toxins, heavy metals from the activities of humanity accumulate in the body and cause problems. Some heavy metals, notably mercury, have no function in the human body and as we are on the journey toward transmutation into light form, they are a serious impediment to bodily ascension.

Mercury also has the effect of poisoning the pineal gland, rendering it inoperable and with the gland that is responsible for perception of the higher spiritual planes shut down, we become effectively imprisoned in this dimension, unable to perceive anything beyond it. Mercury is very toxic, given that there are very vigorous controls on mercury emissions from the burning of corpses in crematoriums. Yet dentists routinely put this metal into the mouths of patients when filling teeth and deny there is any problem with it. However when I went to a clinic to have my mercury fillings removed, the dentists wore full breathing apparatus and I had to wear special clothing to prevent contamination. If these kinds of extreme measures are required when working with mercury, then it raises the question of why it is being put in the human body.

The long term effects of mercury are apparent by visiting old people in care homes who have had a mouth full of mercury fillings for many years and often there is a serious deterioration in mental function. Mercury is a neurological suppressant and prevents the development of new neural pathways in the brain. Thus if mercury gets into the brain tissues, mental deterioration is inevitable. Mercury can also be found in swine flu vaccinations under the name of Thimersal. Thimersal contains methyl-mercury which has no purpose in the human body. Mercury can also be found in some children's vaccines as well as in eco-friendly light bulbs. If one of these bulbs is smashed, then mercury vapours are released, which are very harmful when inhaled.

Mercury also accumulates in the marine environment, originating from the burning of fossil fuels and industrial wastes. The metal is ingested by marine organisms, and is transmitted up the marine food chain, with the animals at the top of the food chain accumulating very high levels of this toxic metal. Thus anyone eating large fish such as dolphin and tuna expose themselves to high levels of mercury. The problem of mercury accumulation in the oceans is so acute, that in 20 years if no action is taken on mercury in the environment, it will not be possible to eat any marine organism without adverse effect from mercury. At the same time, it threatens the long term survival of large marine mammals which would have catastrophic effects on the rest of the marine ecosystem.

So we have an issue where one of the most toxic metals known to humanity has permeated the environment and threatens our long term physical and neurological health, yet little has been done about it, because to do so we would have to question industrial practices that are very profitable and to stop them would affect economic growth. One of the issues that humanity will need to address very soon is the fact that economic growth presides above everything else, even the wellbeing of people and the environment and it is something that cannot be maintained for very long. China, with its economy growing very fast, now has severe environmental problems, with most rivers and soils heavily polluted. A breakdown of the environmental ecosystems in China has the potential to jeopardise the survival of one billion people, almost one sixth of the global population.

My personal experience was that within weeks of having my mercury fillings removed, my consciousness expanded rapidly, the spiritual pineal gland began to function and I was able to perceive previously inaccessible spiritual planes of consciousness. One day I felt infused with light and from then on the bliss never subsided. Clearing the mercury from the body allowed it to detoxify on a deep level and over the coming months I excreted calcified liver stones and all other kind of accumulated toxic debris, resulting in a higher state of healing and wellbeing. I would advise any reader to make to removal of mercury a top priority if one is serious about healing and will let the reader draw their own conclusions as to why the mercury is present in and used by the medical and dental institutions within humanity. It is likely that in the future the use of mercury in medicine will be seen as a massive crime against humanity, and whether intentional or not, the long term effects of this toxicity will be staggering and it will take many years of deep healing to undo some of the damage done.

For weaker people, or those exposed to mercury at a very young age, some of the neurological damage is unfortunately irreparable.

At the same time as removing the mercury, I stopped drinking and showering in tap water, with concerns that fluoride and chlorine also have adverse effects on the pineal gland. Tap water is also treated with all kinds of chemicals. We have no idea what subtle but deleterious effects many of these may have on the human body. The water companies also invariably will only remove chemical contaminants recognised as problematic or will remove them to a so called 'safe level'. However we do not know as yet whether there is a safe level of some of these trace chemicals. Pesticides and herbicides are applied in vast quantities on inorganic farms, and enter the water table. It is most unlikely that traces of all of them are removed from the water supply.

Other chemicals that find their way into tap water include industrial discharges decreed safe, paints, oils, solvents, leaking batteries discarded in streams and rivers as well as a massive array of household cleaners and chemicals deemed to be safe. However these chemicals are deemed to be safe by the same scientific standards that do not recognise mercury to be poisonous to the human body or do not recognise fluoride to weaken teeth and bones, when it has been shown to have the same effect in animals exposed to fluoride from volcanic ash. Humanity will not be able to find deep healing whilst it continues to drink tainted and toxic waters, for no matter how hard we eliminate toxins from the body, polluted water will continually bring in more until the body finally succumbs to illness.

It is very unlikely that nature intended the body to have to deal with so many different modern day chemicals that did not exist as recently as 100 years ago. I believe this cocktail of environmental pollutants is seriously harmful to our bodies and impedes the ascension of our consciousness, as the energies of our being are constantly expended in dealing with the constant onslaught of these toxins. Picking up a conventional cleaning agent or shampoo in the supermarket gives a long list of chemical ingredients, some of them difficult to pronounce and many of them are not found in nature having been created in the laboratories. As well as poisoning our bodies on a subtle level, the majority are also tested on animals in laboratories, where animals are subjected to barbaric and horrific experiments to ensure the safety of humans.

However a lot of these chemical cleaners are totally unnecessary. For many years I have washed all manner of surfaces in nothing other than water and a basic eco-friendly washing up liquid. This same liquid launders clothes very well at the lowest temperatures saving a fortune on expensive washing powders. Long ago I replaced shower gels and shampoos with nothing other than soap made from vegetable oils resulting in an improvement in skin quality and the disappearance of dandruff. Fluoride based chemical toothpastes were replaced with natural alternatives, and many years of suffering through mouth ulcers came to an end. Deodorants are not needed on a pure food diet, which I will discuss shortly, so eliminating the need to spray toxic aluminium and alcohol based derivatives onto the body.

The amount of chemicals we are exposed to is astonishing, and originates from a wide range of sources including; washing powders, toothpastes, gels, air fresheners, household cleaners, DIY chemicals, batteries, sanitizing sprays and gels, mouthwashes, pharmaceutical medicines, pesticides, herbicides, vehicle emissions, swimming pool chemicals and solvents (including Corexit 9500 used in the Deepwater Horizon oil spill disaster). Many of these chemicals are totally unnecessary and for which there is often a natural and simple alternative. Most sanitizers and kitchen chemicals are designed to prevent the spread of food poisoning bacteria, which invariably are found in meat and dairy products and so if these are eliminated from the diet, these chemicals become unnecessary. Humanity has become so obsessed with killing bacteria that the good ones in our bodies are often wiped out too, ruining our immune systems. If we live healthy lives our bodies will have natural immunity to any naturally occurring bacteria, rendering most of modern antibiotics unnecessary and redundant.

It will be necessary for humanity to wake up to this situation and acknowledge that this chemical overload on the environment and our bodies is a serious issue that needs to be addressed. Many of these chemicals become lodged deep in the tissues of the body and though may appear to have no ill effects in the short term, are actually doing untold damage to our health, contributing to the rise in cancer cases and on the spiritual level impeding the ascension of our consciousness. Whilst struggling to find cures for cancers, humanity continues to poison itself with all kinds of chemicals and fails to see the connection.

Removing these toxins through detoxification processes such as fasting, green juicing and the raw foods diet can bring about massive changes in health and wellbeing, but most noticeably once these chemicals are out of our bodies, we are able to perceive the higher realities as the higher chakras of the body begin to function again. With these spiritual chakras closed, we remain in a state of confusion and misunderstanding about our spiritual nature, resulting in a lot of unnecessary suffering. Humanity now needs the higher chakras open to the spiritual realities so as to be able to channel the higher wisdom, love and illumination needed to bring about our spiritual awakening and planetary healing, and it can only be done through detoxification of the body.

Moving on to food, eating the correct food is one of the most important aspects of the ascension process. Only the purest foods will do if we wish to attain higher levels of consciousness and understanding. The best foods are those straight from nature, organic and full of natural nutrition, unsprayed and not irradiated or processed in any other way. The processing and heating of food destroys enzymes and reduces nutritional value. Inorganic farming has no place in the future of humanity and must be abandoned to avoid an agricultural crisis as soils become depleted of essential organic nutrients necessary for continued growing seasons. Inorganic farming often results in a field becoming agriculturally useless after a few years, whereas organic farming can be performed indefinitely on the same land. Inorganic farming also drains soil of nutrition and then renders it vulnerable to erosion. The natural formation of topsoil is a process that takes hundreds of years to produce a couple of inches and inorganic farming can consume that in a few years, threatening a serious looming food crisis for humanity if not addressed.

The population of humanity is growing rapidly and only the most efficient and natural farming methods can hope to sustain perhaps 50-75% of the current population long term. Inorganic farming produces the illusion of being able to grow more, but it is only a short term gain as the subsequent soil toxicity and ultimate failure to support crop renders its benefits illusory and environmentally it is extremely costly. If the cost of the loss of topsoil, chemical contamination of the environment through the use of pesticides and the effect on human health was factored into the price of inorganic food, it would almost certainly be commercially unviable to produce food in that way.

Organic farming produces healthier and more nutritious food and so we can find that we need to eat less of the same vegetable to feel nourished. After a couple of years of eating only organic food, eating inorganic food will cause bodily discomfort and the chemical sprays will be detectable to the taste even after washing the food. Washing the food does not remove all contamination, as some chemicals are applied whilst the plants are growing and are absorbed into the vegetable itself, these contaminants cannot be removed or the plant purified before eating. Inorganic farming is a violation of what nature intended and is deeply harmful to the ecosystem, our health, and our wellbeing. It is also worthy of note that extensive inorganic agriculture has only been made possible by the advent of fertilisers created from the by-products of fossil fuels, a rapidly dwindling resource. It will be necessary for humanity to totally abandon conventional farming practices, if it is to avoid a serious reduction in the ability of the Earth to provide food.

I am sure it is not a coincidence the makers of the genuine crop circles chose crops in which to communicate their messages, for the agricultural infrastructures of today is far from what nature intended and if we are serious about healing ourselves, food is a fundamental starting point. Genetic modification and tampering, the spraying of chemicals, battery farming , harmful processing and preservatives – all of these things must be given up to be replaced with a system that produces nothing other than top quality natural and organic food, directly from nature and not interfered with or contaminated in any way. Humanity remains deep in ignorance for as long as it does not recognise the vital importance of healthy food and it is a gross delusion to think that any amount of economic growth or medical advances can compensate us adequately for the ill-health and lost vitality that results from sustained and systemic poisoning of almost all of our entire food supply with chemicals that our bodies are simply not designed to deal with.

Despite the dubious studies suggesting that organic food has little nutritional benefit over and above conventional produce, it is obvious that uncontaminated food will be far healthier. The inability of the human collective to recognise this stems from a mode of consciousness that places no value on natural food, and this consciousness is created and reinforced by poor eating habits and a separation from our deeper emotional heart centres. When we are in tune with our hearts and bodies, we will never eat in such harmful ways, or support systems of agriculture that are responsible for environmental degradation. When we have love for ourselves and our bodies, we naturally love nature and this in the new humanity will be reflected by the new agricultural systems that arise from the collapse of the old.

So having arrived at the reasonable conclusion that eating organic food provides optimum nutrition and promotes good health whilst maintaining a sustainable relationship with nature, it is then necessary to re-evaluate our standpoint toward the eating of meat. Though there may be a few tribal communities that depend on meat for survival, in many cases the eating of meat is an unnecessary indulgence with severe environmental and health consequences. The eating of meat, results in a much higher land usage per person, contributes to world hunger and increases the cost of food overall. Scarcity of food worldwide could be alleviated by the renunciation of the meat based diet and it is inevitable that at some point humanity will be called upon to make the change.

Cattle farming is responsible for much deforestation. Meat eaters will often claim that it is the demand for soya that creates the destruction, but the demand for soya is artificially high as China buys the majority of it to feed its massive livestock population, rather than consuming it directly. A lot of the Amazon is cleared for cattle ranches. Cattle also require a massive amount of water during their lives and when contrasted with dwindling fresh water supplies across most of the planet - cattle farming is not environmentally or morally tenable.

Many humans eating meat are unaware that the habit is a major contributing factor to world hunger, however eating meat raises many karmic and moral issues that can be a spiritual impediment to a higher consciousness. It is interesting to note that most people with a strong interest in the spiritual life are vegetarians and I believe that the renunciation of eating meat for moral reasons results in a deeper sensitivity of heart towards nature and the planet, which then naturally brings about deeper spiritual illumination. It is difficult to reconcile the spiritual path which advocates minimising suffering to living creatures, and the eating of meat which causes a lot of suffering to animals and damages the environment.

I have witnessed the scenes inside modern day slaughterhouses and it is impossible to claim that the animals are treated humanely. The animals are simply treated as a commodity and are poked at, sliced open and sometimes left writhing on the floor in agony, bleeding everywhere whilst other animals look on in fear. If we are eating the products of the slaughterhouse, then energetically we are importing into our bodies the fear of the animals as well as incurring a karmic debt for playing a part in the unnecessary killing of the animal.

I have seen many instances in my life of extreme animal cruelty connected to the meat industry. If we are to eat meat, at least we should go and look firsthand at how it is prepared and be prepared to kill the animal ourselves and eat it. I believe a lot of humanity is in a state of denial or ignorance about the reality of meat production and are addicted to eating it, even though it is not really necessary. It is well known that vegetarians and vegans are healthier, for anyone serious about spiritual progress, the renunciation of eating meat and the associated dairy products is a fundamental first step on the road to a deeper bodily healing and restoration of emotional sensitivity. To illustrate the lack of healing, sensitivity and awareness that can come about through eating meat, I will share a very short personal experience based on someone I knew.

I was once eating a raw organic salad of colourful vegetables and salad with someone who seemed to think I was eating total 'sh*t'. As a long term meat eater, grappling with long term ill-health and anger, he was unable to tolerate the presence of the food in the room, ironically striking out at the kind of diet and lifestyle that could heal him. Apparently 'I' was doing my health no good by eating this natural food, it was causing delusions (contact with higher beings) and he wished me to be treated by the mental health authorities for receiving communications from higher beings wishing to help humanity !

However weeks later he was admitted to hospital for the removal of a congested and infected gall bladder, which is responsible for the elimination of some of the toxins from the body. The point of sharing this experience is that in some cases, when our body becomes so deeply poisoned from the products of the slaughterhouse, which sometimes are literally contaminated with faeces through poor practices, we lose the ability to recognise the animal products as the cause of the illness. Then we enter into a state of denial and a loss of awareness where even in the face of debilitating sickness one fails to see the connection between poor diet and ill health.

Toxic accumulation in the body often impairs judgement and feeds the addictive personality making the body want more of the food responsible for the illness. For these people obesity, chronic illness, repeated hospital admissions, an erosion of emotional sensitivity and the suffering of a difficult death are all common features of their lives. If we are unable to be effective stewards of our own bodies, then how are we going to be able to rise to the challenge of being responsible stewards of the Earth?

Developing a healthy relationship with our bodies, knowing how to nourish it and keep it pure, thus seems a vital step on the way to planetary healing.

Being vegan is environmentally very sound and has massive benefits for health, but there comes a point where one is presented with issues around the eating of cooked food. Once the vibration of the body reaches a certain point and one attains a high level of healing, then the body will begin to protest and struggle with eating cooked food, even though previously it may not have been a problem. Being vegan for a while will restore the body close to its natural condition and optimum efficiency, after that eating cooked food will begin to overload the system. Cooking food destroys many enzymes and nutrients and for the ascension diet cooked food is close to useless. This method of preparing food can sustain the body for a lifetime and even maintain good health, but there is a higher state of healthfulness and spiritual illumination that only becomes apparent when cooked food is renounced, or at the very least reduced dramatically.

In my opinion, cooked food acts as a vibratory toxin and though ordinarily not relevant, at this time our vibration is increasing rapidly to become realigned with higher spiritual realities, and thus a deeper purification and bodily cleansing is called for. The ensuing detoxification process that the body goes through when one ceases to eat cooked food is extreme for a time. However years of accumulated toxins are eliminated and the body then operates at peak efficiency. Though disputed by conventional science, moving to the raw food diet can cause the body to eliminate hardened black mucoid plaque that builds up on the colon wall, which is undoubtedly the cause of many diseases and it is not coincidental that bowel cancer is common in modern civilisation. When one completes this detoxification, illness is very rare indeed and I am sure that if I had not have transitioned to the organic raw food diet, I would not have been able to receive the communications from the Star Beings. The raw foods diet increases the vibration of the body to the highest levels possible.

For many people, including myself, this is as far as the food journey can go for now although the Star Beings explain that very soon some people will develop the ability to live on the vibrations of Light alone and not require any food. Once the physical body has totally transmuted to Light, no physical nourishment of any kind is required. If this does become common, it will no doubt help to alleviate environmental stresses on humanity. The raw food diet helps to reduce our carbon footprints in that fuel that would be used for cooking is saved. Many types of sprouting seeds, a common food in the raw diet, do not even require soil to sprout, needing only a little water and sunlight and are a very environmentally sound food as well as being extremely nourishing.

Humanity would do well to totally re-evaluate its relationship to food and the environment in order to be able to assimilate the higher consciousness into the collective psyche. A thorough cleansing and detoxification of our bodies and environment is called for. If we do not do this, it is likely we will succumb to disease, ill-health and mental deterioration in large numbers and will become unable to function effectively as a collective. Presently, humanity is polluting the eco-systems with all manner of harmful toxins, with little or no thought given on how to remove them later. Removing them will soon be vital and will become one of the most pressing tasks facing humanity.

The Star Beings may well be able to help us with this task; however we will not be able to receive their assistance without a considerable degree of emotional and ethical maturation. Without the karmic resolution brought about by the maturation, we will not be able to receive the communications from the Star Beings or if we somehow do we will succumb to fear and denial and not wish to act on their instructions anyway.

By cleansing ourselves and the Earth of toxicity we also heal ourselves deeply and heal our connection to Nature. Nature is very deeply healing and can provide us with all of our needs, if we learn to respect it and learn to live with it rather than work against it. Ultimately this is not optional and if we fail to learn how to live in harmony with nature, we may well end up experiencing significant population reductions as the ecosystems fail.

A collapse in human numbers would result in untold suffering, however we are heading toward that possibility and we need to urgently modify our behaviours to avoid this scenario. Speaking of human population reductions seems a taboo subject in most circles, however it is something we all need to be aware of and by doing so we become more self aware and make the possibility far less likely to happen. At the moment, most of humanity is sleepwalking toward a future of environmental devastation with no or little awareness of the possible consequences of its actions. The Star Beings communicate the timescale that we have available to make thorough and transformative change is 10 years from now - at best. It calls for each and every one of us to play our part, we now have a moral duty to examine our behaviours and make any corrections necessary for the benefit of the human collective. We have assistance on hand from the Star Beings but we need to be able to heal ourselves enough to be able to receive communications from them.

Purification of toxins from our being and the environment is a vital part of the process. Purification also extends to the heart, so that all negative emotions and fears are processed and released so they are not an impediment to our ability to love. Attachment to negative emotional stories and fear creates conflict and disharmony and on a global level leads to war. Any war will have collective unresolved emotional issues and fear as well as cultural intolerance as the root causes. When we are all able to heal these issues and develop a deeper sensitivity and compassion toward all of humanity, the age of war will be over.

Not only is there a war raging between peoples of the world, but also there is a devastating war on nature being waged and a deep conflict within as we have become separated from the spiritual source. Only if we can make it back to the Source and reconnect with our hearts, will we develop the compassion and wisdom required to end the outer conflicts and bring about an age of peace.

Chapter 7

Meeting the Star Beings

Having healed fears and moved into higher dimensions of consciousness based on love and light, we then have the opportunity to meet the Star Beings. In this chapter I will share more about the nature of these Beings and their higher dimensional realities as well as what these loving intelligences can teach humanity about love and the workings of the Universe. There are many expressions and depths of love possible. The love experienced when one heals the inner fear is only the beginning point on the journey of fully understanding the magnitude and reality of the higher vibratory dimensions of love and light.

I will also explain how meeting the Star Beings arises not from probing outer space, but rather from turning inward to explore the depths of our own consciousness. By doing so we can make some remarkable discoveries about the nature of consciousness, as well as beginning to appreciate the beauty and understand the complexity of the Universe. So where exactly are the Star Beings?

In the higher dimensions space-time becomes transcended and new laws of physics are at work. With this in mind, most of the Star Beings are not located in one particular part of space. They inhabit a realm known as 'hyperspace', which is an all encompassing reality that can contain many dimensions of existence at once, many of them outside of physical plane reality. Hyperspace includes our own ordinary three-dimensional reality - which is one tiny aspect of the overall whole, and hyperspace can be seen as a continuum or spectrum that incorporates many levels of energetic vibration within it. The 'further' we go into hyperspace, the closer we come to Source consciousness and the more luminous and radiant the planes of consciousness become.

When fully understood, hyperspace is seen as a multi-faceted reality consisting of many different planes of consciousness, but existing overall within a Singularity which carries all forms of consciousness within it. This singularity contains within it all manifestations of reality and all dimensions. I would surmise that this singularity is fully comprehensible by a fully awakened multidimensional being. My impression is that hyperspace is the creation of a very intelligent higher dimensional consciousness, on a higher plane even than the Star Beings and we are on a journey back toward the Source and our creators.

Hyperspace transcends and exists beyond our ordinary notions of spatial reality. Many dimensions of reality finer than our own, exist within higher frequencies of consciousness and can be perceived once one is perceiving hyperspace consciousness. Hyperspace pervades ordinary reality in that a single leaf could contain an entire higher dimensional solar system and a whole civilisation of Higher Beings could exist within the space taken up by a few molecules. In what can be likened to the holes in Swiss cheese, our reality is dense, yet contains many empty spaces devoid of atoms or molecules. In these spaces other dimensions exist, being separated from our reality perceptually but at the same time existing within the spaces in ours. The advancement of human perception through raising our conscious vibration I believe will render these other dimensions visible from this reality. A short extract from my diaries points to

this breakdown in ordinary spatial perception once one
is in hyperspace;-

*Upon realising astral mobility I found myself floating
high and free, several miles above some strange planet
totally covered by water in a totally rarefied atmosphere.
Looking down into the water it seemed to have the appearance of a blue shiny icy surface. Closer examination
revealed within this hyper-dimensional structure cities
and civilisations. Maybe it was the Earth viewed from
another level of being or maybe it was the work of some
other species. One small section of this frozen water could
contain an entire city in miniature; it was like there was
a deep honeycombed matrix of many different levels of
reality visible just underneath the surface. If I could have
held a handful of this substance, I would have been able
to hold a million cities or several planets. Size and ordinary spatial relationship appeared to have broken down
into a new reality.*

Until the consciousness of humanity evolves to render
hyperspace visible and perceivable from this waking
reality, which is possible through dissolving the barriers
of unconsciousness between sleep and waking, humanity
is limited to exploring hyperspace through astral jour-
neying or shamanic work. The astral plane or dream
world is one of the lower planes of hyperspace that can
be consciously perceived through improving dream recall
and by working to bring about lucidity within dreaming.
Lucid dreaming brings about an awareness of the multilayered aspect of the dream world and opens up conscious awareness of portals and tunnels into deeper
realms of hyperspace. One can then use these portals to
explore the hyperspace dimension and meet its inhabi-

tants who often have urgent messages for us as a species, as illustrated by the following extracts from my personal logs;-

The first thing I remember was being on some alien world in the astral plane and there was this strange looking liquid on the surface, like a small stream. There was an alien being motioning me to stick part of my dream body in. I thought well why not just go right in fully. It turned out this river was an energetic out-flowing from a higher dimension, because as soon as I got in this stream with my dream body everything changed.

What looked like a multifaceted shiny snowflake structure came down and entered my consciousness. Each part of this hexagonal star-like structure was folding in upon itself and at the same time unfolding outward too. I realised by totally surrendering to this phenomenon all separations between ego consciousness and the higher realities became dissolved and no longer relevant. There was a deep feeling of profound love and then I was gone from that dimensional aspect of the dream-world.

I then found myself on a huge platform, shiny and metallic, just floating in space. There were many alien crafts leaving and arriving and the occupants were of a golden shiny vibration with light rays emanating from them. It seemed strange that there were so many in each small ship, almost occupying the same space as one another. They were looking at instruments within the ships and monitoring the Earth as well as many other inhabited planets galaxy-wide. Seven worlds, including our own were decreed to be in planetary crisis and this platform was a way station for them to make journeys to the planets in question. I was able to receive some com-munication from them.

"Your civilisation is dying on the third dimensional level. You have exceeded the limits of your eco-system and your socio-economic structures are in danger of imminent collapse. The hearts of your peoples are closed by fear and separation from love, and as such you have closed your-self to a relationship with us and with the higher realities of the Universe. Yet it is these relationships your peoples need to find in order to survive the transition. Many of your species are unable to comprehend the full magnitude of your planetary situation for it brings up too much fear and many are in a dangerous state of denial. As you are able to understand the situation without fear, then you must communicate with humanity and help others make the transition to higher consciousness and ultimately to make the ascension out of your dimension.

The ascension for your species is ultimately about walking alive out of the illusion you have created in your minds, rather than through an unconscious death proc-ess. When you make the ascension, you can be with us on these planes and work amongst the different star systems in the galaxy and living on the Earth plane will no longer be necessary. However for those that choose to remain, as your physical bodies begin to transmute into light form, you will be able to teleport anywhere in any dimension through thought alone and whilst on Earth, you will have full conscious awareness of the higher dimensions."

Next I recall hurtling through space at incredible speed, feeling the divine ecstasy as golden rays emanating from stars were intersecting my being. I saw whole squadrons of light ships emerging from solar coronas having entered the stellar matrix from a higher dimensional entry point.

Faster than light speed I flew through the spheres of countless alien worlds. There were emerald cities of iridescent light, matrices, star gates and tunnels through the centres of planets into yet more dimensions. Slowing down I found myself approaching one of these glorious light cities on some far away world, it stood atop a huge mountain range overlooking a very vast smooth plain stretching out in all directions. There was a tall building that seemed to poke out of the atmosphere itself and it was covered in panels and a strange kind of semi-translucent material.

Inside the structure I looked upwards to see strange machinery all over the walls and many, many beings, brilliantly white with some kind of humanoid form floating about. Looking upwards, I began to rise and different sections of the building were rotating – it was a huge portal system for visiting anywhere in the galaxy.

On one floor, the building disappeared and I found myself in a new consciousness, in subtle spirit body, flying through the centre of stars again and through matrices of incredible energetic light vibrations. Many intelligences rose out of the golden light of the stars to take flight alongside. There were many beautiful feelings and sensations, but as yet humanity does not have the vocabulary to express any of them adequately as it is new territory for us. I found myself on the surface of a star in a globular cluster of many thousand stars, as sun after sun of all colours and light magnitudes rose and set upon this star in a complex interplay of light. I saw shapes emerging from these stars and they were Star Beings, appearing to acknowledge my visitation here.

In the above writing the widespread existence of portals throughout hyperspace is demonstrated and from my experience access to these portals depends on matching the frequency of the astral body to that of the portal. Earlier in my experiences, I found that the portals would be visible but remained closed, until I had cleared some karmic or emotional issue that was responsible for creating a density in the overall vibration of my being. I believe that inner and outer reality are ultimately one and an awareness of the inner, will lead humanity to understand the outer reality to a deeper degree and we will then achieve interstellar travel through the mastery of the energies of the Higher Dimensions.

So, free from physical constraints and limitations the Star Beings are not bound to a planet and instead have a tendency to inhabit stars. With non-physical light bodies they can withstand the radiation and heat from the surface and the interior of stars. They have communicated that stars are not simply balls of nuclear fire, but are complex multidimensional astronomical bodies that exist across multiple dimensions at once and the gravitational forces at the centre of stars can create portals or worm-holes in space time into higher dimensions. They have technologies that enable them to enter the interior of a star and emerge out of another, or even make a journey to the Galactic Core itself.

The beings have communicated they have several nexuses or hubs - the equivalent of a home-world (often a star) where collectives of them gather to channel healing energies toward individual planets or entire solar systems so as to raise their level of vibration and bring healing. They do this to assist in the purification of blockages in the energetic grid of a planet so as to prevent severe tectonic stresses and they have done this often with Earth to mitigate or weaken the effect of an earthquake. The increased frequency of large earthquakes in recent years is due to the Earth attempting to balance out energetic blockages caused by the harmful activities of humanity.

One hub appears to be a star named Epsilon Eridani, around 10 light years from the Earth, making it one of our stellar neighbours. Conventional astronomy will not detect any kind of unusual activity on or around the star as the nexus in this star system exists within a dimension outside of our perceptual bandwidth. However as our consciousness evolves and the perceptual rift between the dimensions closes we can expect to discover other planets orbiting the star that are higher dimensional bodies and are thus invisible at present.

The Star Beings communicate that most solar systems contain higher dimensional planets/spheres outside of physical reality. These 'hyperspheres' have branes within them - higher dimensional membranes, microscopically thin. However these membranes are very energetic and can host a wide array of intelligent non-physical entities from seventh and eighth dimensional realities. Some of these hyperspheres are intelligences themselves, as yet not completely within my understanding, but I have been shown these hyperspheres moving in and out of dimensions, changing form and even being used as a craft to cross vast tracts of interstellar space within minutes by creating wormholes in higher dimensional space, or by entering a star and using the portal at the centre.

These Star Beings exist on various layers of the astral planes and as outlined earlier in my description of hyperspace, numerous planes of astral consciousness as well as planes beyond the astral exist within it. There are also trans-galactic planes where moving between galaxies is as easy as taking a couple of steps.

Humanity will be able to meet all kinds of benevolent Star Beings when it is able to turn inwards and explore the space within. The consciousness aspect of our being is limitless and by becoming more aware of the further reaches of our consciousness we can make contact. As the consciousness of humanity increases, then the astral and physical planes become one and then we will be able to make contact with the Star Beings in outer space. However, the distinction between outer and inner space is ultimately illusory, with this boundary collapsing when we integrate and assimilate the higher forms of consciousness.

Until we have unified this duality, we must look inwards first to meet the Star Beings, before searching outer space. When we explore inner space and realise our true nature as being a manifestation of cosmic consciousness rather than a purely physical entity, humanity will make a quantum leap in understanding and break through the veils that shroud us from the higher truths of limitless consciousness and the ability to incorporate multidimensional reality into our being. Then we make the profound discovery that outer space is not separated from our consciousness and that we are actually the universe, with the starry skies that we see being nothing other than the furthest reaches of our own consciousness.

Nothing can ever exist outside of consciousness or be separate from it, or we could never perceive or know it. If we can perceive something, it must be a part of our consciousness and thus part of us. When this is realised and understood, the mind/matter duality collapses and all is seen as Unified Consciousness. Then all notions of inside and outside also collapse, enabling the separation from cosmic consciousness to be transcended and bringing us back to Source Consciousness.

When we are fully connected to Source, we realise our true nature as an infinite conscious multilayered immortal being with the ability to see into the furthest reaches of the galaxy simply by peering into our own consciousness. Then we move into the new paradigm where perceiving the Star Beings becomes a part of everyday reality and in those spaces we can receive deep illumination, love and understanding from them. The following extract from my logs clarifies and expands upon the ideas communicated in the chapter up to this point;-

Alien dimensions are simply realms of higher perceptual vibration than the perceptual vibration of ordinary reality. After some time on a healing journey, ones vibration can rise higher and as a result one can experience other dimensions through the medium of consciousness.

Higher dimensional realms exist within hyperspace – a mode of reality where infinite energies and multitudes of Star Beings exist outside the realm of human perception.

Entrance into alien hyperspace generally happens as the energy field of the body receives a massive vibratory surge. There may be the sensation of a portal or funnel opening up into spaciousness, and then one will suddenly feel light, without substance and become aware of an inner white star at the core of the being, of infinite dimensional depth – a vision of the Source. It is impossible to fully comprehend all of the dimensional facets of this inner essence of our being as it is so far outside of our normal mode of reality, but in time we will understand.

When we enter higher dimensional space our aura automatically becomes cleansed and the vibration of this essence energy will pour straight through the heart chakra and one can be instantly in a state of pure love, resulting in emotional clarity, collapse of fear based patterns and a connection with all beings across all levels. As we move into this highly energetic vibrating field of glorious light that exists within us, one will become aware that one's consciousness is operating like a deep space receiver and by focussing on a signal one can find oneself in a totally bizarre unexplored alien dimension.

Some dimensions contain 'hyper-bubbles' – spheres with thin membranes in space, inhabited by eighth dimensional brane entities. Streams and pulses of energies emanate from the spheres, entering others and opening up portal like structures on the surface where transdimensional craft can enter and exit into different dimen-

sions above and below. Star Beings up here can zip through time and space with no effort at all, and have mastered higher dimensional technologies such as portal mechanics, transmutation, teleportation and brane habitation. Branes are higher dimensional membranes akin to the surface of bubbles that exist across hyperspace, sometimes across multiple dimensions.

After a few visits to these realms it will quickly become obvious we didn't evolve from any apes, but are descendants of some incredibly advanced and ancient race of Star Being who have a benevolent desire to invite us into relationship and ultimately invite us to go and be with them as ascended beings.

Up here one can encounter very ancient powerful intelligences that can communicate telepathically through symbol and colour. Upon entering into communication with them one may see within the mind a dazzling array of incredibly intricate geometrical matrices or sometimes one may sense the beings close by emanating crystalline colours deep into ones aura. However one experiences these higher dimensional beings – it will be profoundly life changing, for it will open up doorways into previously undiscovered realms of consciousness.

One can feel the love of the Star Beings in the form of auric infusions and if we are very open we can receive many deeply profound and healing messages from them. They can communicate through the heart chakra streams of data which can then be assimilated by the brain and pineal gland. Sometimes the downloading from the Star Beings can be extremely intense and prolonged, even *lasting for a couple of days. Usually this means they are preparing us to do big work. The star beings love us with a magnitude the human heart cannot fully comprehend as yet. The human heart on this vibration can only experience love vibrations within certain bandwidths so to speak, but that can change when we leave the human condition behind.*

To leave the human condition behind, we only need to accelerate the vibration of the slowest moving particles in our body and bring them in alignment with the vibrations of the realm we wish to ascend into. Having said 'only' it is actually a big undertaking as it will involve clearing all fears and karmas, whilst opening to love in order to enable ones vibration to reach a high enough frequency. But when one does, one can instantly disappear from the Earth as there will be no corresponding counterparts in the ascendee vibrating at Earth frequency and we can then take residence in a new dimension in a trans-human form. It is this karma and fear clearing that will ultimately enable some of us to avoid ecological catastrophe and jump dimension, and go to a new world with the Star Beings.

In the run up to ascension there will become a point where the higher dimensions become more real, more integrated and one is in them most of the time. Then one can access a lot of energy, ones kundalini may start to awaken or one may have very deep commune with the Star Beings if we are not afraid and open to the experience. A window will open out onto the Universe and whilst on Earth, one may have the experience of seeing a huge array of alien worlds or portals within one's consciousness. Sometimes a portal may manifest as a very fast spinning circle of very advanced technology and often a Star Being will be nearby to assist us if we wish to enter the portal.

As far departed from this reality as it may seem, one day it will be possible for those of a certain vibration to leave through the portals, become intergalactic spirit walkers and continue an existence in relationship with the Higher Beings outside of the Earth plane. This requires a certain amount of healing, a lot of spiritual work and the transmutation of the human body into light form. All of the portals, machines and other technologies in these alien worlds all operate within the dimensions of light and until we are of a certain vibration, they are simply not accessible or perceptible by us. Whilst there are still unresolved karmas in our bodies, we remain dense in body and bound to this plane. As we take up a path of karmic purification and transformation, the vibration of our body will accelerate and we can enter these finer planes of existence and enjoy increased freedom, love, and the beginning of a very profound relationship with the Star Beings. They will show us as much as we are ready to see as they wish to assist with our Enlightenment, for we are loved and nurtured by them, they wish us to discover our higher dimensional body and release our attachments to the material existence.

These Star Beings can work with us in so many ways. They can transmit higher energies deep into our aura to open up any blockages and bring about a higher state of healing. Experiencing their presence can result in entering a pure love state – as this is their state all of the time. With our consent, they can lift us out of this reality temporarily into a realm of star ships, dazzlingly beautiful

*alien star systems and star portals to the furthest reaches
of the cosmos. Often they take us to the limits of our
consciousness, assisting us with transforming the fear so
we can become ever more conscious and fearless. Ultimately, we will discover a very profound truth – that we
are Star Beings too, that we have simply forgotten our
true nature and become entangled in suffering through
over-identification with physical reality.*

*Do not underestimate the effect on humanity of a mass
discovery of our true nature. It has the potential to heal
absolutely everything that ails humanity. These higher
vibrations, once we become aware of them will become
fully integrated into our consciousness and as a result,
our preoccupation with third dimensional activities will
very quickly stop. Our current ways of being - economics,
wars and all the other manifestations of this realm will
simply cease to be when seen as totally pointless and as a
violation of the realities of cosmic love and higher consciousness.*

*The spiritual vibrations will permeate everyday reality
so totally and deeply that everything we have ever known
or experienced will be replaced by a new consciousness
and new structures will arise that will serve the spiritual
needs of humanity. Old structures such as the global
capitalist economy will fall, initiating a period of chaos
within human civilisation. We need not be afraid as by
this point, if we have integrated higher consciousness and
turned toward the new realities of love and connection to
Source, we will become immune to any kind of suffering
or lack , we will no longer require much food with some of
us developing the ability to feed on spiritual light alone.*

Once we become fully aware of our Star Being nature, we will simply drop our physical bodies, viewing them as redundant and outdated shells, dropping our anchor to this low level of vibration and we can then take astral flight to the stars......................

Many people will ask why they do not have these kinds of experiences and insights and why you? They also ask how they can meet the Higher Beings and receive the healings?

Well, I am not special, above anyone else or a chosen one. I have spent a lot of time working on my own healing and spiritual development and come to this place of spiritual understanding though effort. It requires a lot of discipline as well as courage and an open heart to work through all the aspects of ourselves that keep us separated from the higher spiritual truths and realities. However we can all have these experiences if we so desire, we can all fully heal and recognise the light and so receive the love from these beings. It requires us to re-evaluate all that we have been brought up to believe, to conquer our fears and return to a space of love. If we can do these things whilst avoiding becoming entangled in meaningless material pursuits, one day we will receive the fruits of our efforts.

The fruit of our efforts is to complete the climb up the mountain of consciousness and at the summit, having conquered our fears and self-limitations, we receive spiritual illumination and the higher planes become open and accessible to us. The journey of consciousness is arduous and difficult - however the main purpose of human existence is to complete this journey. The journey from suffering into spiritual illumination is explored in more depth by the following writing, produced through channelled insights as well as reflection on my personal journey of meditation and spiritual seeking;-

The summit of consciousness is reached when the seeking ends with all notions of seeker and the sought disappear into the eternal infinite present awareness. All is love, there is clear vision of the whole path trodden, a sense of enlightenment, deep wisdom and compassion for others. The doorways into other realms of consciousness are then opened for us and we meet the Star Beings.

The spiritual journey up here can be likened to a climb up a very hefty mountain. On the lower slopes one walks through swirling mists and clouds, representing the obscurities and confusions of the lower conscious realities. From here, the path further up the mountain is often obscured and thus one gets stuck and forgets even that there is a spiritual path to tread.

In these mists, many other fellow travellers are also on the same journey and collectively forget there is a path, so engage in behaviours that separate them from connecting to the Source. Most of humanity is here, not sure of the way, not even knowing they are on the mountain as the clouds prevent seeing up or down. Here dense collective karmic patterns play out and suffering is perpetuated through a lack of clarity and love. For some it is too much and they actually end up retreating down the mountain, where lies basal survival consciousness and strong attachment to earthly material life.

This is a difficult place to be on the path, for obscurity and lack of clarity results in decisions and choices being made whilst not being connected to higher wisdom and love. A self repeating pattern then plays out as fear and misunderstandings about reality remain, preventing the awakening of a higher perspective. After undergoing much suffering, one can finally surrender to the deeper purpose and as one opens to the Divine, it is like the sun finally shining through the clouds.

At this point we are reminded that there is a path and one may have a vision of a path much further up the mountain. These glimpses of the Divine – of the Light, encourage and motivate us to seek further and to look beyond the stories of the ego - the control dramas, the hurts, the fears, the resentments that play out endlessly and keep us encapsulated in a limiting and unenlightened consciousness, closed to love and in a space of fear and misunderstanding.

As we are motivated to push on upwards, suffering begins to diminish, and we are presented with a higher altitude landscape of bright sunshine and only occasional mists obscure the path. In these lighter more expansive spaces of consciousness, we can make decisions from more loving and open spaces. By doing so, our karmic pile begins to diminish and we experience far more fortuitous conditions in our lives.

Moving ever upwards, we look down and sees a dense, thick blanket of cloud below where one spent so much time in suffering and confusion. Once we are outside of suffering, the majority of the healing is complete. The sun shines for long periods of time, basking the slopes of the mountain in light. Long sections of the upward trail become visible. It is lonely up here as not many people make it this far on the journey though all carry the potential to do so.

To move on from here, requires a deeper surrendering of ego-self, and the transformation of all subtle fears. Deep seated fears manifest as high altitude storms, threatening to blow us off the path entirely. The path becomes treacherous and narrow, for many spirits it is too much and they begin a descent into more comfortable climes. With courage and determination, we can continue ever upwards, and the sense of dualistic self finally begins to dissolve into a higher unified reality of light and unconditional love. From here, the summit of the mountain becomes visible, motivating us to complete the deepest spiritual work.

By this point, most of our suffering is transcended and we are faced with the final fears that limit most of human consciousness. Here we are presented with our fear of death and the fear of losing the ego self. These are formidable obstacles and manifest on the mountain of consciousness as slippery, ice encrusted pinnacles of sheer rock. Beyond lie scintillating wide open snowfields and the final summit. Many who attempt this final climb often fail and retreat down the mountain to take up a more comfortable life style. However the rewards are high for surviving this final passage, making the climb out of all fears and surrendering the idea of ego self to Oneness.

Up here we can then experience a clear and unhindered consciousness. Fears and self limiting behaviours finally lose their power, we are empowered and experience illu-

mination. Seeing far down the mountain, we understand the journey and thus are able to guide others. We become an instrument of love and wisdom. We make it up here in total humbleness, for the ego long departed and there is only the reality of spirit up here.

Everywhere is fully illuminated and the heart is fully open to the reality of Oneness. In total surrender we feel fusion with the Divine. We have transcended all suffering, seen the causes of suffering and the possibility of a new enlightened consciousness. The spiritual seeking is over, for where else is there to be other than in the eternality and full awareness of the now moment?

The profundity of the final realisation cannot be adequately communicated or conceptualised, for the summit of human consciousness moves beyond any ideas, concepts, or any path. The path was just a means to an end for getting here. One then finds there is no here, there, or one as the final enlightenment is about the collapse of all dualities into naked and fully aware singularity consciousness. There is no longer a mountain, a climber or an ego. There is very little one can say about this kind of consciousness. There is just is-ness – just being-ness, there is no seer, or thinker, or meditator. Just open awareness, freedom, love, awareness of immortality, iridescence and 'naked now' moments.

Completion of this spiritual journey brings about an expansion of conscious awareness, subsequent contact with the Star Beings and a deep, lasting spiritual illumination in which all sufferings are transcended. We also develop a deep understanding of the nature of consciousness. By doing so the final veils that keep our vibration at lower levels are removed. Ego-based consciousness is then seen as an illusion shielding us from the truth of the higher realities. Seeing the light of the higher dimensions brings about deep clarity and awakens the heart. It is the awakening of the heart along with the expansion of consciousness that enables us to see through the illusion of the ego constructed reality which separates us from love.

Chapter 8

Entering into relationship with the Star Beings

It is possible to enter into a deeply loving and intimate relationship with the Higher Beings that is profoundly healing on many levels. The relationship is not sexual, nor does it need to be, for sexuality is a physical plane function and is not required for the expression of love in the higher dimensions. When our hearts are open to this possibility and we are not afraid of them, we can then have a close relationship with them. Their gift to us, if we wish to receive it is a new form of love that carries with it the ability to totally purify the human heart of all negative emotions and unresolved traumas. The characteristics of this kind of love are very difficult to express in words for it is purely an intangible experience, but I shall attempt to do so. The tangible proof that this love exists is in the complete healings that are brought about within people who are in relationship with the Star Beings.

Deep seated traumas and multiple negative emotional complexes that would take years of psychotherapy or counselling can be healed in weeks. The ability to process complex emotions increases when exposed to this higher love and the grief of a relationship ending can be processed properly in a fraction of the time. At the same time childhood issues can be healed rapidly, enabling us to be fully free of them and find full inner empowerment, long before the onset of old age. For if we reach old age with unresolved childhood issues, it is likely they will be so concreted into our being that resolution will be much more difficult and it is likely many of the diseases that stem from them not being resolved will have already done irreparable damage to the body. The new humanity will ensure that its children receive proper spiritual instruction so as to be healed of these traumas long before adulthood, recognising their ability to destroy one's life, health and wellbeing if left unchecked.

This ability to rapidly heal and process emotions does not make us emotionally insensitive and detached, but rather this is the effect of Higher Love in expanding the capacity of the human heart to feel beyond the ordinary realities of normal emotional patterns and relationships. Slow emotional processing and development stems from an attachment to old emotional belief systems and a strong belief in how a loving relationship ought to be. When these beliefs are challenged strongly, unless we have a higher emotional and spiritual perspective we can find ourselves in a protracted 'broken heart space'. When we are able to receive love from the higher dimensions, and integrate it into our heart centre, it will be possible to become a deeply loving being, but at the same time the heart will be strong enough to become totally immune to being 'broken'. There is a misconception in the collective of humanity that we are heart-broken when we love, but I believe we are only heart-broken when we do not fully open to the reality of love and instead become attached. Attachment often stems from dependency and is not love.

We can still have and enjoy what we call normal conventional relationships if we so wish. At the same time the healing of humanity requires us to push forth the frontiers of loving into totally new and uncharted territory, if we are to transcend the fears and confusions limiting the spiritual growth of humanity. Thus our relationships are likely to evolve in many new ways. People may opt to move away from the notion of lifelong unions and instead find growth and love through loving many people over the course of a lifetime. This should not really be seen as sinful (as the Church would have us believe), but rather can be seen as an expression of an ever-changing dynamic of spiritual and emotional development within the lives of human beings. Attempting to put love into a particular 'container' and then force it to comply with that only limits growth which causes suffering and prevents us from experiencing the higher expressions of love which are limitless and free from boundaries.

Most of the rules and requirements of a conventional relationship, for example; exclusivity, lifelong, and having no significant intimate relationships with others often stem from fears of abandonment or being alone, and rarely serve our higher spiritual purpose. Of course, there is a place for commitment in some relationships especially where children are involved, but love calls for us to have the discernment and sensitivity to be able to determine what is best for the relationship we are in and the spiritual development of all concerned. In some cases, moving away from demanding exclusivity, dropping excessive expectation and healing the fears of abandonment - which often stem from childhood, will call for more flexibility and fluidity in our approach to intimate relationships. Being freed of relationship constraints that do not serve the lives of the people involved brings growth and liberation, ultimately enabling one to be more receptive to love in all of its different manifestations.

Love from another human being is beautiful and has value. However it is not the only type of love that can be experienced and by realising that, we open ourselves to the possibility of love from a Higher Source. When we experience Higher Love, we can then often return to the field of human relationships and love in a more mature and spiritual way which benefits all concerned and contributes to the overall healing of humanity.

Experiencing love from the Star Beings is a deep teacher, they show us what love really is and when contrasted with our beliefs of what love is, we see a big difference. Resolving these differences brings about deep healing. For most of human love is tainted with the wishes and desires of the ego and is rarely pure. We often feel we love someone, but also have subconscious or sometimes conscious agendas to control them or to take advantage of them for our own benefit. This is not altruistic and often leads to conflict in families, groups of individuals and humanity as a whole.

The love of the Star Beings can show us, albeit painfully, our shortcomings in loving and when we are shown them, we have a great opportunity to resolve them and move away from ego-centred notions of love into more altruistic, compassionate and purer forms of love. Ultimately we all need to embody these higher forms of love if we are to bring about a deep healing of ourselves, humanity and the planet.

Receiving love from a Star Being is a coming together – a meeting of auric fields. This is extremely powerful and to begin with only the smallest exchange will happen, for the amount of energy it releases is phenomenal and the energy channels of the human body are not as yet fully cleared for receiving extreme amounts of energy from the higher dimensions. Healing processes – particularly those concerned with heart healing, along with optimum nutrition will expand the capacity of the channels, allowing us to experience the higher planes more fully and at the same time facilitating deeper contact with the beings if we wish.

They can also send us love through a channelling – one may suddenly feel their presence within the heart and a sense of total, satisfying, healing and beautiful love. Often it comes with the perception of colours or of golden light. When this happens I often receive mental images of them, rainbow angelic transparent faces, a group of them and they communicate through colour. Sometimes they hold what appear to be shiny geometrical objects made of light vibrations which sparkle, shine and emanate love.

When you have received this love, ones perception sharpens and one also feels deeply touched by what can be described as a divine current that then ripples through the body and heart, bringing about sensations of illumination. Often one will then have sudden clarity about moving forward with an issue in life. With this love often comes deep guidance.

Sometimes their love can be an ongoing experience, in which one receives their communications for days at a time and the kundalini channels become filled with coloured spiritual energies from the higher planes. When this happens one is almost on the brink of leaving the body and the whole of the material reality dissolves and one is presented with the sheer luminosity and expansiveness of the spiritual planes. In these moments of absolute lucidity, one can see to the stars and feel the cosmic vibrations entering the body. I believe these kinds of experiences are preparations for the eventual ascension out of the physical plane. They have communicated that once these higher vibrations become fully integrated into the body, transmutation of the physical body and immortalisation will occur.

When these beings enter your life, healing and communicating in this way, one reaches a point where one feels very deeply loved all the time and one can receive deep guidance and instructions from them. Often they will show you much, if you are willing to be a vessel for light and an instrument of healing. If you wish to help heal others then they will guide you in doing so. I asked them how I could help humanity, and they gave instructions to write this book and give talks. When one follows their guidance, one receives much abundance and ones whole life becomes a joyful and loving expression of spirituality and love.

Contact with these beings is so deeply healing if we are able to move past the fears of Higher Beings. It is understandable when one looks at the way extra-terrestrials are portrayed in science fiction films. We have the Aliens Quadrilogy in which the plot revolves around scary aliens butchering and slaughtering humans in gruesome ways, in what appears to be little other than an elaborate outward projection of our own fears. Then we have the film Event Horizon where those who enter a star gate come into contact with a hell dimension. These films I feel are deeply harmful to the psyche of humanity by creating a fear of beings from other worlds, so when the Star Beings do attempt to make contact with us, we are closed to them and deny ourselves the healings on offer.

However an exception is the beautiful film Avatar, carrying many spiritual and moral messages for humanity. This is the kind of film that portrays extra-terrestrials in a more realistic and truthful way, for in this film the Blues have a deep connection with nature and see it as sacred. When humans are frog-marched back to our ships at the end of the film, this clearly carries a very humbling message to humanity and depicts the current state of our civilisation, plundering, destroying, and killing, with no respect for the Earth or nature. I am sure the makers of this film received deep channelling from other Beings and the producers have done a superb job in raising awareness of the behaviour of humanity and of what can be learned from Higher Beings and from respecting nature.

It is easy to realise that extra-terrestrials of any form are unlikely to be a threat to us, when we realise that to enter space requires a massive degree of global cooperation. To form a space faring civilisation along with all the necessary technologies would surely require a massive amount of collective effort and unity so as to be able to draw in all the necessary expertise. It is also likely that there is nothing we have that they would wish to take from us – after all we have plundered the Earth's resources and damaged the environment to such an extent, that our own existence is now at stake. It is highly unlikely a highly evolved race of ETs would wish to take our planet in the condition it is in.

The biggest threat to humanity is from ourselves, our own demons (in the form of fears and unresolved karmas) and by not being willing to work with them we instead project these fears outwards into the cosmos. We then become frightened by the idea of space invaders, aliens, spaceships and the like. When humanity processes and clears this fear of Higher Intelligence, we raise our consciousness and pave the way for mass open contact with them, which will transform humanity beyond recognition and lead us out of dangerous, damaging ego-based behaviours that stand to wreck the only habitable planet within perhaps twenty light years of the Earth. Humanity needs to be able to live on a planet properly and then prepare to leave the Earth, for both practical and spiritual reasons.

However to be able to leave we need to firstly develop a responsible attitude toward the planet we have and then work to heal and restore it. It is unlikely that we will be assisted by the Star Beings to find and damage another pristine planet. However if we show signs of spiritual and moral maturity, I believe we will be shown ways of living beyond the Earth and receive all the assistance we need to do so. The coming years present different opportunities depending on our soul choices. For some we can remain on Earth or colonise the Solar System in the third dimension and for others we can leave this dimension entirely for the higher realms of existence. Whatever option we choose or have chosen, the age of limited ego-based consciousness on one planet is almost over. The new humanity is set to enter into open contact with many different species of Higher Beings across many dimensions. A deeper description of the possible future of humanity will be explored in a later chapter.

To be fully able to enter into relationship with the Star Beings as well as clearing the fears around opening up to them, it is necessary to have completed one's own relationship healing or at least the majority of it. This calls for any old issues or patterning around relationships to be identified and transformed. This raises the vibration of the heart chakra and creates the conditions for them to be in contact. A deep sensitivity in the heart is also called for - otherwise one may often miss their presence, especially at first as the contact begins subtly. This relationship with them is always optional and so we will need to invite it in some way to bring it about. If we wish it, then we simply need to have the desire and an open heart for it and by their grace and compassion, they will come to us and enter our lives.

In the same way as an Earthly relationship brings up issues for resolution, a relationship with them will do so too and they will be the deeper issues that prevent us from fully perceiving the higher dimensional planes. If we consent, they can guide us through a series of processes where our deepest fears can be brought into awareness and healed. They can also teach us deeply about humility, for a strong ego will be dissolved by their presence and if we stray too far away from humility into the realms of ego again, they can bring us back home to the heart.

Whether we as individuals choose whether to enter into relationship with them or not, humanity as a whole needs to begin a purification of heart so as to be able to develop the sensitivities, compassion and wisdom needed to move us forward into a more sustainable age. The following channelled writing talks more about the higher forms of love, and why it is so needed today.

Our capacity to love will be deeply expanded at this time of great change. The heart chakra of a human being is a multidimensional vortex of energy that can directly receive infusions of Divine Love straight from the Source itself. The higher heart is capable of infinite love and compassion for the entirety of creation.

We do not feel this and the heart of humanity is so troubled because we have lost our connection to the Divine and forgotten our true nature. We have become entrenched in this reality and come to believe that this is all that exists. As a result, humanity has closed itself off from the infinite source of divine love that is a natural expression of the cosmos. Blocks have become manifest in the heart chakra of individuals and humanity - as a result we find ourselves loving in more finite and limiting ways, if at all. The hallmark of divinity is oneness and with that forgotten, we perceive ourselves as separate from others. The ensuing perception of duality then reinforces notions of self and other, creating fears, misunderstandings, disharmony and disconnection from the healing, unifying power of Divine Love.

Divine Love exists as pure vibratory energy on higher dimensional realities and is a very healing, transformative force. It is also unconditional, in that it just is and is not dependant on anyone or anything for its continued sustenance. It is infinitely self-replenishing, coming from the Source itself. It never began, nor can it end, as it exists outside of space and time in a non-linear manner.

The healing of individuals and the whole of humanity ultimately will come about when divine love is able to enter our heart chakras on this level and do its healing work on us. Usually opening up to Divine Love is optional, however as the Earth is now moving into a field of higher vibrations our hearts also will be lifted into the higher dimensions and love from these levels will attempt to enter our being. If we are blocked, the energy will still attempt to come through and as a result blocks will gradually or suddenly collapse within our heart chakras instigating a healing crisis as we are called to look at alternate realities. We will also be called to look at our fear and the investment in the belief of a self which keeps us in limiting cocoons, insulated and separated from the love of the divine.

Our notions of love will then be brought into question as an influx of deeper energetic vibration ripples through our heart chakra. Undiscovered chambers of the emotional heart centre will manifest into awareness as the process of transmutation begins - the transmutation of the human heart from being rooted in three dimensional realities to taking root in a new higher dimension of awareness. If we are open to this process, many beautiful phenomena will manifest at this time as light rays from the higher dimensions will take the form of light beings, orbs, fairies or sparks and they will move around within our heart, illuminating, guiding and healing.

We will then feel loved by the beings and become an instrument of love from a higher source. In these spaces, conventional notions of love collapse, seen as self limiting, restrictive and incomplete. New expressions of love begin to sprout, take form and flower within the heart.

Notions of equality, compassion, deep respect, oneness and healing begin to permanently establish themselves and we are called to become an instrument of love, moving through the world, going where it is needed, doing what is called for. Often we may find we need to go back and do some peacemaking or some other aspect of personal heart healing before we can move more fully into these more expansive spaces but it is worth the work. Most individual heart work is about learning how to expand into new territories of love, and about practising forgiveness. To be aligned with love from higher dimensions animates ones being, sending healing vibrations throughout the entire being and outwards lifting the vibrations of people around us. We may then feel a deep love and connection with the heart of humanity.

Higher dimensional love offers great hope for humanity which is about to enter a stage of spiritual crisis. The awakening of the higher heart chakra of humanity can achieve much in a short time, even in the face of global upheaval and crisis. It is the closing of the higher heart chakra of humanity that is ultimately responsible for the separations, the dualities, the misunderstandings and the wars.

The heart of humanity will be called to awaken as we are presented with multiple issues on this dimension and ultimately the only way out of the predicament we are in is to recognise our spiritual nature. By doing so we become transformed and are then able to play a part in the healing of humanity. Humanity needs much healing at this time as families are separated, wars rage, people are dominated and enslaved by dictators, and we have lost our relationship with nature. The ascension period will instigate a massive healing crisis in humanity as all the blocks in humanity become manifest at once, calling for resolution and transcendence. It may well be a very intense time emotionally and spiritually for humanity. The old ways that no longer serve will begin to give way and crumble unleashing deep fear within the psyche of humanity as the old world gives way, with nothing appearing to take its place. The reality is that there is a replacement – the embodiment of the higher principles of unity and love, however before they can be fully integrated, we have to look at what has separated us from them in the first place.

As a result, for a time there will be the possibility of chaos as humanity is plunged into its own self created fear and for many there will be no explanation as to why everything we have invested in so deeply has suddenly collapsed around us. Humanity, now well out of its comfort zone will be right in the fire of transformation.

The 2012 period marks the end of the old cycle of consciousness and the beginning of a new creation cycle. Everything that is outdated and outgrown must be cast into the fires of purification and transformation. This is the final and most intense healing crisis facing humanity as six billion of us struggle to rediscover ourselves in the face of environmental and socio-economic catastrophe, as new realities begin to emerge on this planet. The chaos can be overcome and civilisation remade more sustainably, although it requires humanity to surrender to and bring itself in accordance with the universal laws. When one lives in accordance with the laws of the universe, there is peace, abundance, understanding and wellbeing.

Humanity has attempted to build a civilization which goes against the principles of Oneness and universal laws – propped up by economic systems that are unsustainable and benefit only the few. Industries are polluting the planet and squandering natural resources, resulting in mass extinctions of animal and plant life. With total disregard for nature and the Earth itself, we are now a species out of control, in that we now cannot control our numbers. These numbers have massively exceeded natural carrying capacities and without re-evaluating our relationship with nature and with the universe, the extinction wave has the potential to affect us too and is predicted to result in a dramatic reduction in human populations over the next 50 years or so.

However this is not the only future that awaits us. There is another possibility, of remaking our relationship with nature, healing our species on a global as well as an individual level and allowing divine love to begin its healing work on our civilization. If we do that, much can be achieved in a short time, catastrophe can be avoided – yes we will still have to feel the effects of some of our actions, but love is a great purifier of negative karmas and so the effects can be massively reduced.

Love is a great unifying force which has the capacity to bring people closer so as to work together to bring about the transformation in consciousness. Ultimately we all have an individual responsibility to begin our healing work, for healed individuals contribute toward the formation of a healed world. Humanity is now presented with a great opportunity, to raise its vibration, realign itself with love and to repair the damage it has done to nature. If we do so, we will have much assistance on hand from the Star Beings – all we have to do as a species is acknowledge that we need assistance and we will receive.

Asking for assistance is the big lesson for humanity, a lesson in humility and transcendence of the ego. We are not in charge of the Earth or the Universe and once we can collectively acknowledge that, we can begin the healing and change our destiny. Our destiny was always to be a race of immortal divine beings, transcending death, celebrating oneness and infinite love, enjoying a deep and nurturing relationship with the Cosmos and forming civilisations built on those principles. It is still possible, but time is short now.

When humanity is able to surrender attachment to ego and allow the Higher Beings to step in and help us, we will receive much assistance and love from the higher planes as we begin the work of transforming our civilisation. The more receptive we are to expanding our consciousness, being in our hearts and allowing beneficial changes to happen to our systems and structures, then the smoother the transition will be. No human being has to suffer at all, for all suffering is brought to us by our own decisions to move away from love. Coming back to the heart can be very healing and can achieve much karmic resolution. Even in the midst of global upheaval, it can make a difference. The extent of chaos we will experience as we move forward into a new era will be dependent on each and every one of us, and our willingness to engage with the heart, to promote and spread love and to demonstrate compassion and sensitivity to others.

Ways of living based on fear, control and violence must now be relinquished for the common good of humanity. As more of us open our hearts, the collective vibration of humanity increases, carrying the power to heal many conflicts and bring an end to wars. There may be a few isolated pockets of intense fighting globally over the coming years, but the new consciousness will bring an end to most of it as the people involved finally realise the futility of it. However some of humanity may wish to hold tightly to the belief that violence and war is justified, for these groups, karma may necessitate death in a final catastrophic regional war of some kind. It is unlikely there will be a global holocaust; however a regional war may still be necessary to balance out the remaining karmic debt for some groups or nations.

The Star Beings also will have the ability post 2012 to interact more with our dimension as the energetic frequency of the planet increases and the star gate portals become active. This will permit groups of Star Beings to enter into the battlefields and war zones in an attempt to bring final closure to outstanding conflicts and also to bring much needed love and support to war torn ravaged communities ruined by years, or even decades of war. It is in these areas that much healing will need to be done, for ongoing conflict is very damaging to the human heart. However even for those who have lost all of their loved ones, the loving vibrations of the Star Beings can bring about deep healings in these people.

However this does not exempt us from playing a part in the healing too. When the Star Beings become visible, they would hope that we are already well into the job of sorting out our issues and healing our planet. It may be that humanity is morally deficient for as long as people are suffering whilst other people in the world are engaging in excessive material pursuits with no care or sensitivity for its effects on others. The moral fibre of humanity is in need of deep healing now. All impurities, fears, corruptions and all instances of humans inflicting suffering on other humans must now be transformed if we are to become a more loving race. Ultimately the spiritual growth and progression of humanity can only be done in unity. When the divisions and conflicts in humanity are healed, then the resulting energy of conscious unified intent can bring about a lot of change in a short time and bring about all kinds of solutions to global issues.

At the moment, the collective psyche of humanity is fragmented and not integrated, with different groups of people pulling in different directions with no underlying spiritual purpose. Today the only common purpose appears to be maintaining economic growth, which only benefits a small minority of humanity. If we are all to benefit, it will need to be relinquished for a higher ideal. When love, rather than money, becomes the driving and unifying power behind our civilization, progress will be rapid. When driven by love, we will not rest until everybody is free from suffering, everyone has enough to eat, feels loved, nourished and free from persecution. We will continue to work until the environment is totally restored to its original pristine condition, free from toxicity and pollution. All of nature will be respected, preserved and allowed to be. When we live in harmony with nature, we will be deeply rewarded with the most nourishing food and the healing that comes from a sustainable relationship with the Earth.

It is a massive job that we have to do now as a species, but really it is our only option if we wish to avoid a future of environmental and societal degradation ravaged by conflict. At the same time, the power of love should never be underestimated and as we heal on a deeper level, this increases our capacity to think clearly, wisely, lovingly and compassionately. We will then know what actions to take at what time to bring about the healing of others. It is contact with the Star Beings and the higher forms of love that they express that I believe will finally bring about a deep healing in the heart of humanity. For the processes involved in order to be able to receive their love necessitate the resolution and abandonment of fear, the moving away from an ego-based consciousness, a thorough purification of being and a return to the heart centre.

At the same time, when the love of the Star Beings is experienced, it humbles us, and puts us in our proper place - which is abiding in the heart. We may think we are in control of everything - however we are not in control of the situation on Earth and we are losing our ability to maintain a sustainable relationship with nature, which ultimately stems from a deep separation from the heart leading us to act in all kinds of harmful ways. Unless we are able to be humbled, and surrender to the egoless wisdom and love of the Higher Intelligences, I do not believe we will be able to heal ourselves sufficiently to avoid catastrophic suffering and a breakdown of humanity as the consequences of our actions begin to have full effect. It is only a return to an illuminated, heart based awareness that can bring about a strong enough motivation to begin the healing work on

Earth before it becomes too late. It is worth remembering that love is a very strong karmic purifier, and many consequences of our actions can be mitigated in a very short time, if we are able to purify our hearts and see what we have done to ourselves and the planet.

Chapter 9

Into the Higher Dimensions - Alien worlds and Cities of Light

Beyond the physical plane lie the realms of the Star Beings. A spiritually awakening human being will have conscious access to these dimensions, and one who heals all karmas and develops a mastery of living in three dimensional realities has the opportunity to move into those blissful and illuminated realms permanently. Existence in the higher planes, free of physical form and the necessity to take rebirth in these lower realms, is the next evolutionary step for a significant percentage of humanity. Free of physical form, one transcends space and time limitations, and becomes an immortal Star Being. We always had that capability, but our inner luminosity became enshrouded in the denser vibrations of this reality, and shrouded by confusion, fear and doubt we lost sight of our true nature. Over a long course of human history many of us have come to believe we originated from this Earthly dimension as descendants of apes and monkeys.

Inner luminosity is the higher dimensional aspect of us that contains the light body. The nature of the light body is trans-physical, weightless, indestructible, immortal, eternal and hyper-energetic. When we live in this dimension, it becomes imprisoned and we lose conscious awareness of it. However, through spiritual and healing practices we can regain our lost awareness of it and through raising our vibration it becomes free and able to take flight to the stars and other heavenly dimensions during sleep, shamanic work or meditation. Our level of vibration will determine to what extent we will be able to astral travel in sleep and in any case it will be necessary to have healed the fear of death to prevent the astral body simply hanging around the physical, afraid to move away for fear of not returning. Recalling our astral adventures into these higher dimensions is greatly facilitated by the detoxification of the pineal gland of heavy metals, fluoride, chlorine and pesticides.

Ultimately the light body is our true nature and all that we are, for the outer shell of the physical body is not permanent and breaks down at death. Rebirth results in the creation of a totally new body, and so the only aspect of our being that remains intact throughout the life-death cycle as well as the higher ascension processes is this inner light body. The light body exists across a spectrum of many dimensions simultaneously and there are many layers of light body awareness which become manifest as we raise our vibration into higher realms of consciousness.

Freedom from the physical form is granted upon resolution of all earthly karmas. For those who learn the lessons of spirituality and love, and play their role in the healing of humanity, a new opportunity will be presented – one of leaving the Earth through ascension out of matter. The human body, simply being a physical manifestation and a result of past karmas, becomes totally transmuted at the moment of total karmic purification. Karmic purification usually takes many lifetimes, but the acceleration of the vibration of the planet presents a rare opportunity now for full purification in this lifetime. The higher dimensional energies that filter into our auras once every 26,000 years make this purification and subsequent ascension in consciousness possible.

In the light realms the matter/wave duality that exists in this dimension is transcended and intelligence can take on the form of pure wave essence. The light realms are based on different temporal and quantum laws, and things not possible in this reality become commonplace there. Existing in two places at once, entering the centre of stars, faster than light travel and intergalactic communication are all possible here. There are different intelligences on various levels of the light planes, all are benevolent and it has been communicated to me that some of the highest reaches of these planes are beyond the comprehension of any human in this dimension, so a full understanding of the entirety of the structure of the spiritual planes is not possible for now.

Dimensional ascension is a process whereby all spirits return to the Source of consciousness. My experiences have shown me that the human race is currently at a stage of evolution where the source of origin appears to be the Galactic Core. It is doubtful this core is the ultimate Source and at this point in our evolutionary journey, speculation as to whether there are other Sources beyond the Core has limited value, so we would do well to focus on our current journey. However, the sheer number of Galaxies with some of them emitting extremely intense radiation, along with the fact that ours is not the largest or special in any way, may imply some galaxies may consist of higher spiritual frequencies and that there is a further journey beyond. What astronomy picks up as intense radiation from the Galactic Core, I believe are also higher dimensional energies that we can assimilate into our being to raise our consciousness. If our bodies and hearts are open and pure, then these energies can aid in the acceleration of our consciousness and through my experiences in hyperspace appear also to be calling us back to the Source.

The Star Beings communicate that Galaxies are complex structures that exist across eight dimensions and that the black holes at the centre appear black because our consciousness is not raised high enough to perceive the higher dimensional light emitted from the vast interdimensional portals that exist there, therefore we see or detect a black void. On the spiritual planes, the so called Galactic black hole appears to be a massive white Super-Sun. Our Earth's orbit around the Galactic plane means that we can receive emissions from it every 26,000years, and be recharged - dimensionally speaking. This recharging allows the possibility of integration of, and alignment with higher dimensional energies allowing for an ascensional jump once we are cleared of lower dimensional 'baggage'. Entering the Galactic Core results in ascension into tenth dimensional consciousness - a realm within hyperspace that exists above the Galactic Dimensions that permits inter-galactic travel.

The centre of our Milky Way galaxy appears to be the entry point into these dimensions from where myriads of souls appear to enter and exit some Grand Central Galactic Sun, the source of all spiritual luminosity in this galaxy. A vision of this Central Sun is depicted in the following writing from my blog;-

After some time in the realms of light, one wonders where this light actually comes from. The Source of the light is beyond the astral planes, within the galactic dimensions. At the core of our galaxy is a huge star billions of times the size of our sun, existing on a higher dimension and thus not visible from Earth. However conventional astronomy can pick up the intense radiation

being emitted from the Galactic Core. This central star is the portal out of our galaxy, and is the Source itself. Whether it is the end point of our spiritual journey is open to speculation, for many other galaxies exist, some of them existing on higher dimensions than this one but no-one as far as I am aware has ever been beyond the core and returned with any information.

As we develop the ability to journey further through the astral planes, one begins to approach the source directly and we can become dazzled by an incredibly intense luminosity. This light can burn away many impurities from the heart and auric body. Billions of individual spirits can be seen entering and emerging from the core as tiny migrating specks of light, almost insignificant against the backdrop of the magnitude of the Central Sun. Many times we can come here and be turned back, for it will not be possible to enter the Central Sun in spirit form until we reach a very high level of purification and consciousness. However, seeing it is useful and even at a distance it can transform us profoundly and deeply. This Central Sun or Source is also intelligence, vast, profound, all knowing, wise and deeply loving. It wishes us to return. This is possible by completing our healing and purifying ourselves of all negative aspects that are not in accordance with the Light. Then we develop the ability to venture closer to the Central Sun and to receive more of the healing vibrations. The closer we get, the easier it becomes.

Healing the fear of Higher Intelligence is deeply important for us to come here. As we approach the Central Star an inner light also rises from the core of our hearts and one may have the vision within of a million suns rising *above an infinitely expansive ocean. This is the recognition of inner essence / inner luminosity and an orientation toward the Source. Entering the corona of the Central Sun, many intelligences emerge, transmitting a vibration of ancient wisdom and deep love. At the same time, vast structures appear. Spinning, rotating structures, incredibly advanced technologies, created from light and having no physical form, they pulse, hum, buzz and move at speed with purposes unknown. Some of the light-ships are designed to enter the centre of stars to emerge elsewhere out of another. These intelligences exist permanently in the highly energetic vibrations of the corona of the Galactic Central Sun, as they have the ability to harness these incredible energies.*

The surface of this giant star appears to be covered with a membrane of rainbow light and the circumference of this celestial body is unfathomable. At this distance, it is impossible to see the curvature, as it is so large. There are portals here, entering into the centre of the sun. Huge tunnel like structures appear to go deep into the star. The whole of it is alive with ever changing manifestations of light and technological complexity. Buildings appear to exist on the walls of these tunnels – huge towers and cities of light, positioned at what appear impossible angles. Bubbles, beings and ships emerge from the buildings, with some flying off into space and others entering the stellar core. The energies emerging from these cities are the communications from very powerful intelligences with the ability to transmit the communication across the entire galaxy.

When we become spiritually receptive we can receive and interpret these communications – they heal and awaken our multi-dimensional star-seed consciousness and call us to begin our journey home to the Spiritual Source. Healing our fears of other-worldly beings opens a window onto the Cosmos, and we can be shown visions of our ultimate destination, the departure from suffering, a complete healing, the transcendence of death and the return to immortality. In the meantime, it is this awakening in consciousness that will expand and purify our hearts, opening us to the deepest love present in the Universe. Having experienced it, we can then turn toward the healing of the human race and of the Earth, so that all may become enlightened, healed and free from all fears. For there is nothing to fear, for we are all loved by a myriad of benevolent intelligences, we can be free of all suffering and we can all make it back to the Spiritual Source. No-one is separated from the Source forever (as Christianity would have us believe in its messages of eternal damnation in hell for the non believers).

The Galactic Core appears to have the ability to be very healing when approached in the spiritual dimensions, as well as being a vast cosmic intelligence that seeds and supports a wide array of other intelligences. The complexity of technologies surrounding this Central Star is way beyond my full understanding, but I would surmise they are the work of deeply spiritual beings able to live in such proximity to a massive energy source. Three dimensional human beings do not have the ability to live so close to any star, for our physical bodies cannot handle the tremendous energies being emitted. My feeling is that the emissions from the Core have a purpose in the sustenance of all life, and no planet or being can survive for long without infusions of this energy. The energy from the Core streams through our Sun and we then receive it. This may well be the cause of the intense solar activity currently being seen as our own star receives higher-dimensional recharging, with the flares being the Sun's attempt to integrate this very powerful energy.

It is likely that the vibratory frequency of the entire Solar System is being raised by the infusion of fresh energies from the Core. This raises our vibration and may well act as a cosmic purifier of lower, negative vibrations of being. This purification can bring about deep healing on an individual and planetary level, but will also be the main cause of the massive coming healing crisis, for some of humanity will not be prepared for or able to assimilate these higher frequencies, with intense resistance to the new consciousness causing illness and death.

The purpose of this cosmic recharging is to bring about a deep healing through an awakening of our higher dimensional DNA strands which are not visible under the microscope, but once activated reawaken the dormant light body. Science has determined that 98% of our DNA has no value and is therefore labelled "junk DNA". However this so called junk DNA contains the blueprints for the activation of our higher dimensional light bodies. These DNA sequences can also instruct the body to purge itself of all toxins, and can also awaken distant memories of past lives and visits to other dimensional realities as well as details of one's spiritual purpose in this lifetime.

The awakening of these latent strands along with the visitations by the Star Beings are the cause behind the healings and spiritual awakenings we are now seeing worldwide. To assist this process it is vital to attain a level of bodily and emotional purity, so that denser blockages do not impede the awakening. Heavy metals, notably mercury, have a tendency to interfere with and delay the activation of the latent DNA strands. Once these strands begin their activation sequences one's reality begins to change and one begins to perceive multiple or parallel realities, as well as being able to receive higher dimensional communication from the Galactic Core.

One way we can receive information from the higher dimensions is through a phenomenon known as carrier waves. Within the complexity of multidimensional space, informational waves weave through and between dimensions and realms and intersect with our aura. These waves carry communications from Star Beings in the other dimensions. At the same time these waves are composed of a very subtle multifaceted light that has effects on the energy body, healing, revitalising and rejuvenating. The content of these carrier waves once assimilated will bring about the birthing of new realities that become established and permanent. One is able to 'see' in new ways, as the ability to see each higher dimension is integrated. One can be open to this as there is nothing to fear at all, with the experience being very liberating and insightful.

Signs that this is happening will be the awareness of many strands and matrices intersecting our being emanating from elsewhere. There may be other-worldly imagery such as intrinsically dynamic and complex geometrical formations within our awareness. One may have the experience of seeing other star systems, or huge spinning rainbow funnels leading elsewhere in the multidimensional scheme of things. Ones whole life becomes infused with an ecstatic, loving and divine awareness of a deeper mode of being. We realise then we are deeply connected to a source that emanates healing vibrations throughout the whole of multidimensional reality.

Without this regular energy influx from the Core into our solar system, our spiritual light bodies would degrade and break down. The light and cosmic radiation near the Core is too energetic for our current energy bodies, and hence in our evolution we find ourselves in a system two thirds of the way out from the Core. A massive degree of bodily transmutation is required to live in the Galactic Core – to the point where beings of that realm are made of pure light and nothing more.

The increase in the emanations from the Core and the birthing of a multidimensional body also gives rise to the realisation that our Earth and our own chakra systems contain portals. In our chakra system they manifest as rippling deep tunnels within our being. Often the Star Beings will appear alongside the portals, and download information into our being about using them. They are predominantly a means to visit other dimensions and ultimately leave Earth completely, if we so wish as the rate of our bodily transmutation quickens. The bodily portals appear intimately connected with the planetary portals and form an inter-dimensional network within planets in this system. They also lead to other star systems – Alpha Centauri and beyond. The energetic frequency of our light bodies is increasing and at a certain point our vibration acts as a portal key and we will be able to use the portals. Intrepid travellers will then be able to travel to other stars, meet a whole range of highly evolved and benevolent Star Beings and ultimately ascend into a new vibratory reality.

So the main spiritual task facing the light workers on the planet now is to draw into this reality the higher dimensional energies so as to bring about the awakening and transformation of consciousness as well as a collective awareness of higher dimensional realities and truths. This instigates the main passage of healing – the aforementioned healing crisis. After this has passed the remainder of humanity left on Earth will become multidimensionally aware and will have an awareness of other realities whilst being on the Earth. This will mean that what today are seen as farfetched notions will become commonplace. Everyone will receive and understand the communications from the Galactic Core, all will be vibrationally attuned enough to see the higher dimensional beings as well as having the ability to use the portals.

A collective awareness of the portals will enable humanity to become multidimensional explorers, developing the ability to journey into hyperspace in waking consciousness and visit other star systems - dimensions of pure light, communing with light beings in beautiful light cities on hyper-spheres spread throughout the Galaxy. We will be fully healed and grounded here on Earth, yet the higher dimensions will be available for us too.

From 2012 onwards, as mentioned previously, a number of people will leave the Earth entirely through the portals as their spiritual obligations to humanity will be completed – namely bringing about the awareness of higher dimensional consciousness in the collective. For these people, they will become permanent residents of the higher planes and can opt to live in any one of the light cities, or become a cosmic healer working with other planets that are in crisis and thus will be able to explore the cosmos at will. A vast amount of possibilities exist for those who cross the vibratory threshold completely and drop their body. Never again will they be forced to take rebirth to learn difficult lessons, but they may choose to incarnate on other planets in crisis to be of service and to bring about awakening there. Most of the time they will be part of a collective of Star Beings in one of the cities, just one aspect of a massive alternative realm of existence extending across many dimensions.

The cities of Light are partly accessible to those with a degree of astral mobility whilst on Earth and are the abodes of the Ascended Beings. Some of these cities can be found on other planets in higher dimensional regions of space outside the physical and some can be found on the surface of hyper-dimensional membranes within hyper-space. Most of these cities are translucent and emanate a lot of light, so much so that they are often inaccessible to Earthly astral travellers until a high degree of healing is attained. Suffering does not come anywhere close to these cities as they are manifestations of pure love-light consciousness.

The buildings within, though without physical form take on various ethereal forms and often appear to stretch to impossible heights above the city in long needle like tower formations. A particular light city has massive dome-like structures not dissimilar to jellyfish and out of the domes crafts can be seen leaving. Sometimes the whole city exists within a coloured translucent bubble, but this is not always the case. The vibrations emanating from these cities are very strong and appear to have the purpose of filtering the healing energies of love and light down into the lower dimensions.

Usually the collectives within these cities operate as a whole, existing outside of our notions of duality. Though there are still individuals within the collective appearing to do different things, the underlying unity between them is unbroken, all act with common agreed purpose and so there is continued peace and harmony. Up here, when you are in a space of love and light, there is no desire to do anything to undermine or destroy that. Sometimes the beings here are all white, sometimes they have a rainbow hue and they can all move incredibly fast, taking on various forms. In one experience several of these beings came together, created a bubble around themselves which took on the function of a craft and zipped off, stopping later over a tall precipice, with the bubble craft opening out into segments, disappearing and leaving the rainbow beings standing there.

There appears to be a technology up here that can create star craft in the form of multidimensional hyper-spheres. These hyper-spheres act as huge transit craft for entering star portals. They consist of many outer membranes that can peel away or dissolve into multiple doors allowing the beings or other smaller craft within to emerge, leaving an inner core of the craft intact. They *appear to have the ability to create crafts as an extension of their consciousness and have created some incredibly advanced technological constructions made out of ethers alone. These crafts and technologies appear to harness the cosmic energies of the light vibrations.*

The intense gravitational energies of a star on the matter-plane appear to create eddies and vortices in the higher planes that can be used to move from one dimension to another with the use of these hyper-sphere crafts. The higher dimensions contain the higher dimensional light bodies of the stars (all stars are sentient intelligences) and these higher dimensional aspects of the star connect with those of other stars across six and seventh dimensional hyperspace enabling instant transit between any two stars in the galaxy. These star portals also appear to create passages into 'brane-bubbles' where even higher dimensions exist beyond stellar hyperspace. These dimensions appear as shimmering reflections on the surface of massive bubbles that interact with each other and they also have strange looking cities on their surfaces.

Huge space stations also appear up here and simply through a boost in our vibration, our consciousness can shift from the Earth plane and we can awaken in hyperspace in the midst of some technological creation made by the Star Beings. These space stations are often found in orbit within the coronas of stars, and some lie close to the Galactic core itself, and teleportation devices within allow for transit between different stations. Though the intelligences are very benevolent, they are surprised to find human consciousness appearing up here. There is no need for any security or guarding up here, for our con-

sciousness will let us see anything we are attuned to seeing and so it is not possible to hide anything on the higher dimensions - for anyone with the corresponding vibration will be able to see it. Hence these realms are intrinsically open and transparent – being open and transparent on the Earth plane may well contribute to the ability to visit these higher realms.

These orbiting stations pulsate and vibrate with light, there are many panels and instrumentation. This all exists within the ethereal realities, having no solid sub-stance. The floors are often decked out with hexagonal panels with patterning similar to honeycombs and marked with varying unintelligible inscriptions and alien writing. There is a strange sound in these places, almost like the sound of metal cymbals vibrating long after they have been struck. The vibration pulsates through the chambers and brings about a sense of familiar recollection as if one had been here many times previously. Many of these stations exist up on the higher planes and have varying purposes, the ones I have experience of seem to have the role of monitoring planets in crisis and the Star Beings have helpers in human form, who can then be brought back up to the station in spirit form to receive further information, assistance or instructions. The Star Beings saw our crisis coming long ago and sent almost half a billion people with experience in helping planets in trouble to incarnate here at this time to assist humanity. Humans are descendants of various Star Beings - some are conscious helpers in the current crisis whilst others came here to resolve personal karmas.

The scope of these light realms is beyond comprehen-sion and there are huge arrays of intelligences every-

where, sometimes taking on the form of huge matrices that look like hyper cubes except they have more dimensions in them than a standard hyper cube has. Beings in these arrays can interface with the energetic fabric of the universe itself and as one penetrates deeper into these realms, the arrays give way to bubbles and hyper spheres made with rainbow light. On one level, our three dimensional universe can be seen existing as a bubble against a backdrop of millions more and wise, loving intelligences oversee the whole thing. It becomes obvious that many of these higher intelligences can create the conditions for life, a new planet or even a new universe. When we look at their translucent forms, where we would expect to see a heart, we see a multitude of coloured rays and bubbles that extend to encompass the whole of the dimensional spectrum. They are bringing the latent energy and power of creation into existence simply by directing the energies of love and light.

There does not appear to be a single creator up here, nor is there any conventional notion of a God. It appears there are many creators and that after the journey of dimensional ascension, we too have the possibility of becoming a creator. The important message behind all of this is that we carry the innate ability to know directly through experience the creators of our reality and we can become one of them through conscious evolution and ascension of consciousness. The false sense of separation created between the Divine Creators and humanity by the founders of the Christian Church, the cause of so much existential suffering and confusion, is then recognised enabling humanity to rise out of the mindset of inferiority and the entanglement in dogmas. For centuries humanity has been led to believe we are totally inferior beings in the face of the Creator and that direct spiritual experience is not possible and when it is experienced, it is shunned or negated. Seeing through this illusion offers the potential for humanity to resolve its existential crisis and find a true, deep, spiritual understanding.

These experiences of higher truth and reality can heal the heart of every human being of all existential sufferings and shatter the illusions and bondages of religious conditioning that has done nothing but to enslave the heart and spirit of humanity to a false belief system. At the same time these institutions threaten those who challenge or reject those beliefs with the fear of eternal damnation. Seeing the higher realities and experiencing the love of the Star Beings can heal all fear, rendering this power game played by the religious institutions ineffective. Free of fear, no-one can be scared or manipulated into any religion or institution. If we find ourselves in one, then we have vulnerabilities in need of healing that these fear-based institutions have exploited.

There are many pure teachings in all of the world religions and they have much to offer humanity, but it is vital that we have the discernment to separate out truth from the institutional nonsense. By doing so, we avoid falling into confusion and becoming involved with an institution with a dubious agenda. It is possible to receive a full healing and spiritual enlightenment without committing to any world religion. Ultimate Truth and deliverance from suffering is accessible to anyone who can cut through the thickets of illusion and there are many spiritual tools and methods for achieving that. Respect is required for all faiths and traditions, but at the same time part of our necessary healing is to make sure they respect you - if they do not then it is unlikely they will bring you any closer to spiritual enlightenment.

There is no punishment delivered upon us by a judging God, the only aspect of judgement that appears to exist is our own higher consciousness which has full conscience and discernment to see all actions from a pure perspective. We are made by loving intelligences to be creators of our reality and as we evolve we become co-creators of the Universal Reality. The love of the Star Beings, the Creators or the Divine Beings (however one wishes to label them) is available to every human being regardless of religious persuasion or belief. We are all made of the Spiritual Light and no one religion can determine who and who cannot have access to it. For the Divine vibrations of the universe are what we are all inherently made of, with that in mind we all have eternal life and no one can ever experience eternal damnation by not following the limited dogmas of one particular religion.

Spiritual truth and the experience of seeing the light is a universal experience that every human being can experience. Mistakes in the interpretation of the experience and the manipulation of the Truth to serve the agendas of those who wish to enslave and control humanity have brought about a ridiculous amount of unnecessary suffering in the heart of humanity.

To see the light in this way is beautiful and enlightening. That in itself is profound, and re-evaluates our relationship with the cosmos. But the deeper significance of these experiences is that they liberate us from all fear and confusion, and by coming face to face with cosmic love we can be cleansed of all suffering, restored by the light, and be spiritually reborn. In this place no-one can ever control our spiritual destiny, and it is through the experience of receiving the love of the Star Beings we are made strong in heart and spirit. Strong in vibration, aligned with love, we can them become an instrument of global healing and transformation, shining the light to others, so they too may make the final ascension out of suffering.

Chapter 10

Humanity's Healing Crisis

As the healing process continues in humanity, it is likely that a period of chaos (a healing crisis) will be experienced in which all that needs resolution in humanity will be brought to the fore at once. The coming purification will split open the heart of humanity to reveal whatever is within. If there is love, then that love will shine forth with strength and light, however if there are wounds, resentments or agendas harmful to others or humanity as a whole hiding inside, all this will be clearly visible for everyone to see, and so some segments of humanity will undergo a difficult healing process.

The heart of the human collective and the individual stand to be totally purified of all that stands in the way of the arising of a higher love based consciousness, and so the spiritual purpose of the coming healing crisis will be to purge greed, hatred and ignorance from the psyche of humanity. If we have already done a lot of this work, then we will experience little suffering and instead undergo a massive transformation, acceleration and ascension in consciousness. For those who have not, this is the time when one way or another all these karmas (unresolved issues) must find resolution.

I believe this healing crisis has already begun, both on a global and individual level, with the ongoing problems in the global economic and environmental systems and as I write the oil spill in the Gulf of Mexico is still spewing massive amounts of oil into the sea with untold future consequences. At the same time large numbers of individuals are experiencing personal difficulties as many long standing fears and unresolved emotional issues are finally rising to the surface calling for resolution. Individuals are also experiencing disillusionment as modern day life has failed to bring a sense of deeper peace or happiness and are increasingly turning to spiritual groups in an attempt to find some deeper meaning to life.

A healing crisis is the period where latent unresolved issues come up for resolution and when there are several, it often precipitates a period of chaos in one's personal life until resolution is found and one is able to move into a higher state of consciousness. Likewise, a period of chaos is also unavoidable globally as there are multiple issues in the collective of humanity in need of resolution. Chaos need not be feared, for it is simply part of the process of transformation. When the collective issues are resolved, the chaos of the healing crisis will subside, and a new order will arise based on love and spiritual values.

The duration and intensity of the coming healing crisis will be determined by the number of people in the collective still carrying fear and other unresolved issues, and the readiness of humanity as a whole to embrace change. If a large number of individuals can complete their healing processes now, before the main crisis in humanity begins, then the transitions will naturally be gentler. Those who have completed their healing processes prior to the transitions will be able to act as guides and helpers as they will be able to stand fearless and loving even in the midst of turmoil, chaos and intense suffering.

In this healing crisis there is an opportunity for purification as all of our karmas can be purified in a single lifetime. Usually karmas play out over many lifetimes, but with the movement of the planet into higher vibrations of consciousness, this karmic baggage cannot be carried any further and must be unpacked now. This is why life is becoming very intense for many people and much is being called for from every individual. People are being asked to go to their limits and in those spaces undergo transformation and complete healing, as well as working for the betterment of humanity. This is an opportunity for everyone to wipe the karmic slate clean and start afresh.

At the end of the purification cycle – when the movement of the Earth into higher vibratory reality is complete, the karma of every person will be resolved. It can be done through conscious healing, through the suffering of a difficult death or other major misfortune or through engaging in selfless service to humanity. It is this karmic purification which will finally draw an end to this age of suffering and confusion on Earth and carry us forth into an enlightened age of peace, understanding and open contact with the enlightened Star Beings.

Every human being now has the option to choose a path for their individual purification and karmic resolution, as well as choosing the way they wish to heal. Voluntary engagement with the healing process avoids the necessity of intense suffering later in a period of global healing crisis. We all have issues that we need to address within ourselves and the amount of suffering we need to experience in order to find resolution is dependent on our willingness to face ourselves, move away from fear and to embrace change.

For those open to new possibilities, it can be a time of transcendence of the ego-self, illumination, freedom from suffering, an increase in wellbeing and great creativity as new modes of consciousness are integrated into ones being. Abundance and love will then naturally flow into one's life. The spiritual truths will be readily assimilated, understood and there will be no need for further suffering as all karmas find resolution. For those more resistant and determined to hold on to fear and control dramas, resolution can only be found in the intense suffering of global upheaval. Anyone can walk out of suffering at any time, but once the upheaval begins, physical and environmental conditions may become unfavourable and one's reactions to these can create further negative karmas deepening the suffering.

It is likely that those who have healed themselves will be guided to safer and more stable locations on the Earth as the final healing crisis begins. The most intense places to be are most likely to be large towns and cities, and in those communities most dependent on the old systems. It would be wise for every person now to face themselves and engage with their healing, to become less dependent on the economic systems and to re-orientate their lives to be in alignment with nature. Natural diets and ways of living will all help to make the transitions smoother.

The period of healing crisis offers the potential for massive transformation within humanity. It will also be the time when the structures that no longer serve the spiritual interests of humanity will collapse and we are likely to see huge breakdowns and upheavals in the political and economic systems. In the rest of the chapter, I will explore the different aspects of the upcoming chaos, the systems likely to fail and how we can make it through the transitions.

The first thing important to stress here is that humanity has exceeded the carrying capacity of the planet. Natural resources are limited and agriculture can only sustain a certain number of people. There also needs to be room on the planet for the rest of nature to exist alongside us, for many of these plants and animals play a vital role in the maintenance of the eco-system. Humanity does not yet understand many of these roles and by destroying nature we may well bring upon ourselves catastrophic consequences.

Without nature in balance and functioning correctly, our time on this planet can only be limited. Our population is still growing rapidly and many people across the globe are aspiring to live a Western lifestyle which is inherently unsustainable. With the above in mind, it is likely that humanity will very quickly come up against natural limits and without an immediate attempt to reduce population or consumption, some kind of collapse in population is inevitable.

Reductions in human numbers are necessary to some extent, in order to bring our population back down to sustainable levels. If we are free from fear of death and are aware of the necessity to live in harmony with nature, this will be seen as necessary and accepted gracefully. We have taken far too much from the Earth, and to gracefully accept a reduction in our numbers is to honour nature, and to make way for other species to rebuild their populations. The Earth needs a period of rest and recuperation after the intense activities of humanity and so many spirits have opted to leave through death in the coming years to wipe their karmic slate clean, easing the burden on the Earth's ecosystems.

To continue with our Western lifestyles and not contemplate this possibility is absurd given it is the only likely outcome of continued economic and material development. Many students will know that when bacterium grow rapidly in solution, they eventually consume the entire agar, die off and drown in their own waste products. Humanity is in the same scenario, rapidly consuming resources, polluting the planet with waste products whilst struggling to provide itself with ample clean unpolluted food and water. We may be far more complex creatures than bacterium, but as we require food, we are subject to the same natural law. The same dynamics of population growth and reduction we see in the natural world are thus also applicable to us, should we grow beyond natural limitations.

It is likely that a collapse in human numbers will provide a massive spiritual opportunity for us to see beyond the limitations and illusions of the material plane, to wake up spiritually and to raise our consciousness to the point where leaving this reality is not an issue. Knowing that we have an immortal existence beyond the physical plane, we will see the reduction in numbers as necessary for the Earth and for nature and in a space of total acceptance, will not become frightened or shaken by it, nor will we resist it. We will see it as part of the natural biological rebalancing process. In retrospect the population contraction, however it occurs, is likely to be our greatest spiritual teacher. The contraction will teach the importance of humility, love and compassion in the midst of the suffering experienced by over a billion spirits making a difficult passage from this plane.

For those who hold tightly to material ideals and the belief in this life alone, who do not wish to be open to a spiritual existence elsewhere, the passage will be a traumatic one and there will be much need for compassionate and loving assistance. The departing spirits in the population contraction will also be playing a role in teaching those remaining the importance of a conscious effort to stabilize human population in the longer term. It is likely that a population contraction of anything between 20% and 50% of today's numbers will be required to balance out our effects on nature, resolve our karmic imbalances and to move forward into an age of sustainability.

Some of this reduction will be brought about by conscious ascension of spirits from the Earth plane through vibratory healing and immortalisation, allowing them to leave for other dimensions. This means of departure will be free from suffering. Some of the reduction will be made up of those who will have to resolve their karma through death and a difficult passage from this planet, as outlined in a previous chapter. These two means out of the Earth plane are probably already laid out for some of the individuals involved depending on their level of healing and their karma. However a large shift in consciousness could enable other individuals to change their fate and choose a more favourable outcome.

There are some habits that are extremely unsustainable and the renunciation of these will massively negate the effects of the human population crash, resulting in a smaller contraction and allowing more to remain on Earth after the ascensions. The eating of meat is the one practice globally that if given up could mitigate more than anything else the effects of a large scale population crash. As much as meat-eaters protest that their actions are not harmful to the planet, the reality is that the Earth cannot support a carnivorous diet for all, and save for a limited number of remote tribes, a return to the vegan diet will be necessary to make the best use of remaining agricultural land and fresh water resources. Given that the most likely cause of an increase in human deaths will be through lack of food and water, the giving up of the meat diet is the most compassionate thing we can do to reduce suffering to other humans, as well as animals, and will allow a greater number of us to remain on the Earth.

Another issue connected with the carnivorous diet is that the Earth is moving into a higher vibratory reality. The higher dimensional vibrations entering our bodies from the higher planes to bring about healing and ascension create a lightness of body and spirit that the meat diet cannot support. Most of the diseases in the Western world are a product of the eating of too much meat and dairy products, and if we have these diseases it will be very difficult to move into a higher form of conscious existence. It is likely that as the vibratory energies of the Earth increase, those still eating meat will succumb to these diseases and with their bodies unable to assimilate the new energies, they may find their health deteriorates to a point where death soon follows.

The purification of the Earth and of humanity will probably require anyone wishing to remain in a high state of health and wellbeing to renounce the eating of meat. For a long time, this habit has poisoned the bodies of many of us, clogging up our digestive and circulatory systems, whilst ravaging our immune systems through the ingestion of excessive amounts of antibiotics pumped into the flesh of battery farmed animals. It is something that will have to be renounced to avoid mass human suffering. For many, it will be painful, and some may refuse to stop eating the animals even in the face of terminal illness but I believe it is the only option we have as a collective if we wish to enjoy a sustainable relationship with the Earth, whilst enjoying a state of health and wellbeing. We will never be able to find peace and health, if we are living our lives dependant on the suffering and exploitation of animals and nature.

On an individual level, I foresee that as the healing crisis begins in humanity, those still eating meat will be presented with many physical and emotional difficulties caused by the ingestion of toxins and the karmic effects of being involved in the suffering of animals. For those willing to move to plant based diets, there will be an opportunity for deep healing, detoxification, purification of heart and a shift in consciousness. For those who choose not to, karma may necessitate the protracted suffering and death by an entirely preventable Western disease, such as heart disease or cancer. These diseases are the deeper and final consequences of unhealthy habits or unresolved emotions and in my experience many people die from these diseases in suffering and in fear. This suffering is totally avoidable through re-evaluating our lifestyles and behaviours.

A visit to one of the many care homes worldwide will present the reality of the suffering of terminal illness and death. Many are being spoon fed the standard meat diet in their last days and having it washed down with fruit squashes fortified with aspartame (which breaks down in the body into formaldehyde and wood alcohol, both extremely poisonous substances), whilst suffering the final toxic effects of eliminative and circulatory congestion. With their physical bodies overcome by toxins, their hearts have slowed down and become filled with fear, whilst emotional tensions have turned to physical rigidity and their minds fogged with years of neurological toxicity are unable to comprehend what is happening. This kind of departure from the world is undignified and totally unnecessary – in the new humanity many people will die with a full conscious awareness. To die with a full conscious awareness gives us the ability to navigate the afterlife dimensions free from confusion, so making the process far less bewildering, frightening and traumatic.

The coming healing crisis will also present difficulties for those who use alcohol, or are trapped in other addictive patterns of behaviour. Invariably, the excessive use of alcohol or drugs is often an attempt to cover up a deep wound within and one requires the drug to become emotionally numbed to avoid having to face the underlying issue. Alcohol in anything other than the smallest amounts is a poison to the body as the yearly death rates due to alcohol related illnesses in society testify. By failing to recognise our unhealed wounds and falling into patterns of addiction, we abuse our bodies on a deep level and become totally desensitised to other people. In these spaces, we can cause suffering and hurt to other people, as is so common where alcoholics abuse their partners and children - causing the heartache of family breakups, and these people often then go on to succumb to their illness and have to endure a difficult death.

Alcohol gives the illusion of having a good time, however the millions of people worldwide who drink in bars and nightclubs are often achieving nothing other than a temporary release from the suffering of their everyday existence and the next day the hangover brings them painfully back to reality. Unable to address the underlying issues, the pattern repeats the following weekend and can continue for years, robbing the people concerned of a more meaningful and emotionally fulfilling life. If anyone disagrees that alcohol is harmful to the vibration of the planet, we can visit a town centre after the nightclubs have emptied out and we may well see brawling, fighting, people vomiting in the streets, being bundled in the back of police cars for public disorder offences and the like. The atmosphere is distinctively unpleasant and rowdy and is unlikely to contribute to harmony or planetary healing.

Alcohol inhibits the awakening of spiritual consciousness and thus it is necessary to renounce it if one wishes to make serious spiritual progress. Healing from alcoholism and other addictive behaviours comes always from identifying and resolving the core issue, and facing what one is unwilling to face. The damage that alcohol does to the heart of humanity is extreme and if we as individuals are engaging in behaviours that desensitise us, then this will affect the ability of the collective in finding the sensitivity and insight required to solve many of the major problems facing humanity. It is likely that alcohol will have no place in the new humanity, will be viewed as an extremely antisocial activity. It will be widely recognised for the destructive physical and emotional poison that it is.

For those engaged in addictive behaviours, the healing crisis will call for them to address the underlying issues. For those unable to, it is likely they will descend deeper into their addictions and meet the only end that lies there – intense suffering, sickness and death. For those willing to look at themselves deeply, this period offers an opportunity for deep purification, healing and a release from the suffering of addiction. Often this will require a healing of childhood issues and developing a love for oneself. In that space, one would not think of engaging in physically or emotionally toxic activities, and free from addictions we are able to be fully conscious of the present, and are able to reach a level of healing high enough to be able to become conscious of the spiritual realities.

It is likely that the coming healing crisis will purge out of the collective all addictive behaviours, only those able to find a complete healing from them will be able to move forward into the new consciousness in wellness and free from suffering. Many who choose not to give up these patterns of addiction will enter a phase of extreme suffering during the purification period and will have the choice of healing or death. There will be no third option of carrying on the behaviour and avoiding the karmic consequence, for now all our karmas are coming forth for immediate resolution.

As well as the purification on an individual level; transforming fears and harmful behaviours, renouncing harmful diets, healing our hearts and relationships, there will also be a healing crisis within the collective as the institutions built on fear, greed and confusion finally collapse to make way for the creations of the new humanity. It is very likely that the monetary system of the planet will totally collapse at some point in the very near future. It is a system built on inequality and does not serve the spiritual development of humanity. Based on a belief that bigger is better, it will finally reach its own limits and when there are no more natural resources to fuel the ever increasing levels of economic growth, a massive contraction is inevitable.

Given that the whole economy is now dependant on the moods of the financial markets, even a modest contraction of say 5% globally would render the stock markets value as zero, initiating the final crash. The financial system has been perpetuating a big lie - in that the social and environmental cost does not need to be factored into economic models. However the reality will soon become apparent and when the environmental and social costs of modern day economic development are factored in, it will undoubtedly cost more than the value of the entire global financial system itself.

The banking system will never be able to survive this realisation, for their existence and size has been made possible through the perpetuation of the lie. Resistant to regulation and control, despite having been given billions of dollars of taxpayers' money to save themselves, their greed will finally bring about their demise when it becomes manifest in the collective of humanity the amount of damage they have actually done to society and our planet. It will be seen as a system that extracts as much wealth out of the common person as possible, with full government backing, giving little or nothing in return, either to society or to the environment. Humanity must renounce the banking system and collectively demand that these reckless, ruthless and greedy institutions be removed from the world stage. They only have one aim, endorsed by government and that is to get bigger, and that aim comes at the expense of humanity.

They have enslaved us into a distorted, unjust and warped economic system that has no bearing on the spiritual reality of abundance for all. Being a gross aberration from spiritual truth and ethical standards, they will stop at nothing to attempt to take all the wealth for themselves. This dream of being able to get progressively richer with no limits comes at the expense of bleeding humanity of all spare resources. This will ultimately bring about their demise for they will have no option other than to print more money resulting in the devaluing of their own currencies. The game is over for them, the wolf is at the door and their days are numbered. Though the collapse will be chaotic, it will bring about our liberation.

The whole banking system is built on debt and the bankers can only maintain their power by creating more debt by lending people more 'fictitious' money, which is created electronically and exists only in a computer memory, or in the minds of investors as speculative value. Yet this illusory money then requires hard funds in repayment, with interest added. It is worth remembering almost all of the value of a bank is not based on hard currency, but is based on speculation. If a bank is thought to be able to do well, share prices increase and the bank's value increases, but this speculative value is rarely supported by an equivalent in hard currency. This is what allows banks to lend far more money than they actually have and thus they have needed government money to bail them out. As a bank does not see a value in limiting its size, lacking ethics and conscience, the lending will continue until all of the wealth of humanity is controlled by them or they collapse by the effects of their own greed - and in the meantime millions of people will have lost their life savings, investments and houses.

The mortgage system is simply a corruption whereby the only way to buy a home is to borrow the money from a financial institution and then pay back three or four times the house price over the course of the loan. The greed of the banks and building societies has led to them lending buyers more, which then artificially inflates house prices, making it impossible for many to buy a home in the first place.

Very soon all the corruptions and lies perpetuated by the banking industry will all come to the surface and along with the realisation that the whole global economy is unsustainable, the financial bubble will finally burst catastrophically. The consciousness of humanity is rising, so it will not be possible to hide from the collective consciousness the truths and underlying dynamics behind the global financial system. This collapse is necessary for the wellbeing of humanity in the longer term, but in the short term may well cause some extreme chaos. The reality of the higher vibratory dimensions is that there is abundance for all, the spiritual awakening of humanity will bring this awareness about and it will become very obvious that the global economy was nothing other than a scheme to keep people in a space of lack and need when really there was enough for everyone all along.

When the system collapses there will be a shift of wealth away from the elite toward the common people once a new system is created out of the ashes of the old one. The bankers or governments will have no part in it, for by this point we will have awakened enough to see what they have done and so we will not allow them to participate. It is likely the new system will be based on barter and exchange of goods on a local level, and it will be a love based economy with strong values of equality, respect for nature and sustainability.

The collapse of the old economy will be total and the banks will never open for business again. The cashpoints will simply shut down and no-one in the financial sector will have a job. Virtually every large corporation world-wide will become bankrupted overnight. The leaders may attempt to bring in a new currency, but it is unlikely we will let them. The collapsed currencies will be totally worthless – money saved in a bank will be worth nothing, if you could withdraw it. Surviving this event will be about knowing how to form community, find or grow food and developing local ways of trading that do not require hard currency.

In these times, the balance of power will shift away from the elite to the common people - where it should be. Individuals will be able to form communities, they will become strong and will be the bedrock of the new humanity. This will be our work, to reform ourselves after the financial collapse, to bring our civilisation back into a simpler, more sustainable and loving place. We will have the Star Beings to help us later on this journey, for soon they will become manifest in this reality once our level of consciousness is high enough.

With the collapse of the economic systems will also come the collapse of the world governments, for they are intricately linked and one cannot survive without the other. Many high ranking officials in governments have held posts in corporations and vice versa, and all the harmful environmental activities of the world's largest corporations have received full backing from the government. As they have given the banks bail outs without our consent and then charged the balance to us in the form of future tax rises and austerity measures, it demonstrates their lack of respect for us.

With the financial system gone, the governments too will lose their power and there will be nothing they can do to restore it. They may well go around shooting a few people or threatening to put whole nations of people in prison for civil disobedience, but in a post-collapse situation, everyone will know they supported the banks and corporations all along and very few people will support them. However with the collapse of the governmental institutions, most, if not all of the main players will be overcome with fear and will most likely become ill very rapidly, and will no longer be a threat.

It is worth remembering that the higher our vibration becomes, the less we are likely to draw negative events toward us and if we are free from fear we will not draw into our lives the perpetrators of the fear based agendas. On the highest level of healing, we are untouchable and cannot be harmed by the dark forces. We can only draw harm to us if we are still carrying darkness within ourselves and thus rather than worrying about the agendas of the dark forces, we would be well advised to heal ourselves of our own fear issues. It is possible to raise the vibration of one's body high enough so that a bullet can pass through it without causing any damage, to walk across a battlefield radiating love and not draw any injury, or to receive guidance from Higher Beings so as to move out of the way of any impending harm.

Making it through the global upheavals with minimal suffering, is thus about healing oneself of all impurities and unresolved issues, becoming more conscious and aware of the Light and moving away from all fear into a love based consciousness. Totally rooted in the light and karmically purified, we will not be part of the story of collapse, suffering and death, and for these people there will be great abundance and deep spiritual awakening. As we purify our karmas and awaken, we draw into our being from the spiritual dimensions abilities and skills previously unavailable to us, the number of these we can draw on increases exponentially as we continue embodying more Light. These abilities give us the strength and awareness to deal with all kinds of challenging situations, so when we are presented with upheaval or a difficult situation we will know in each moment how to act.

Some of the abilities we can awaken within ourselves are the ability to see forward in time, receive precognitive messages and guidance from the Star Beings, and the ability to heal ourselves and others energetically without recourse to medical services. We will also be able to interpret our dreams fully which contain many instructions on how to act and which choices to make in our lives. Many of the messages and instructions come from the Star Beings, working behind the scenes, helping us to awaken and giving us the help they can to raise our consciousness and bring about global healing. Soon we will be able to meet them directly in the waking consciousness, but until then the guidance can only come through the dream plane or through intuition.

Never underestimate the ability of an open fearless heart to deal with any difficulties presented to you and in this space you can bring about a rapid healing in those around you. The period of chaos has a spiritual purpose in that all that stands in the way of a higher consciousness can be cleared.

I advise any reader not to succumb to fear when reading about the possibility of chaos. The intention is not to spread fear, but to bring awareness to the consequences of our actions so that we may understand how they have come about, why the collapse must occur and how we can be prepared for the transition period. Everything that happens is ultimately for our highest good and everything that happens brings about growth. Now is the time to put fear aside and develop an aware responsibility for the situation we are in. Having put fear aside, you can then become a loving individual channelling light into this reality and one becomes an active and conscious participant in creating the new future, which will be much different than that which it is today. This is the time when whatever your heart and spirit desires will become manifest, once the shackles of fear and doubt are removed. The next chapter will give some insights into the possibilities that lie ahead for the new humanity.

Chapter 11

The New Humanity takes shape – Open Contact

When the healing is complete on all levels, the new humanity will look very different in many ways to what it is today. The eventual outcome is not fixed, and is dependent on our actions and the intent we have in our hearts to bring about change. However, one thing is certain and that is that the future of humanity will involve open contact with numerous collectives of Star Beings, which will transform humanity profoundly and bring about a final maturation of consciousness. As well as exploring the effect on humanity of open contact with Star Beings, I will explore some of the other changes we are likely to see in humanity in the near future (from 2012 - 2025AD) – environmentally, economically and politically, once the period of healing crisis enters into full swing.

The following is one possible portrayal of the future however it is subject to change depending on our collective actions today. Reductions in populations are very difficult to predict accurately as there has been no precedent in the history of humanity. Many complex factors are involved in the collapse and transformation of an oil and money based civilisation. A rapid spiritual awakening in humanity can avoid much suffering and make for an easier transition.

The Star Beings arrived in 2012. From the start of the millennium, many sensitive individuals were aware of their presence in higher dimensions and from 2009 many individuals were able to enter into deep relationship with, and receive communications from them, however they were still not generally visible in the physical plane.

All that changed in 2012, as the Galactic alignment process had finally completed and had created a total alignment of the physical and spiritual planes. Previously unseen energy portals on the Earth became visible, notably at the sacred sites, the Pyramids, Stonehenge, Glastonbury, etc and shortly after the 2012 winter solstice the first group of luminous rainbow light beings emerged from the portals to greet humanity in the physical plane. It was like the gates of heaven had opened and Star Beings, angels, devas and other higher beings descended upon the Earth, and they quickly set to work on healing people.

Light ships were able to emerge from the portals and for those receptive to the Star Beings and free from fear, they were able to experience open physical contact for the first time. For some humans, their spiritual work on the planet was complete and they ascended out of the matter plane through the portals, some going through with the Star Beings on the light ships. Others of lower vibration tried to enter and were unable to, remaining on the Earth's surface.

For a few people, including most of the global elite, their lower vibration meant they were not able to see the portals or the Star Beings and thus perceptions of reality rapidly diverged with some people literally disappearing without explanation, and with others experiencing rapture and bliss with no obvious cause. However most of humanity now had the ability to see the Visitors, and for them their lives were to be transformed beyond recognition as time went on. At the same time, the appearance of the Star Beings triggered the final collapse of the Old World and the healing crisis began. Some humans were able to ascend and avoid the chaos, but many were to remain and the Star Beings then stepped back and allowed the healing, transformative processes to begin. Within weeks of first contact, the final breakdown and collapse of the structures built on the old consciousness began in a process that would take a few years to complete.

Approximately 10% of the global population raised their vibration high enough to ascend out of the matter dimension and left in groups from 2012 onwards, simply disappearing out of matter-existence through the portals. These individuals, in the run up to their ascension and departure from the Earth became completely healed and began to radiate visible rays and haloes of coloured light from their bodies as well as exuding great love and compassion. Attaining full multi-dimensional consciousness, they became immortalised and their bodies transmuted into light form. Prior to their departure they were able to attain great feats of healing and acted as spiritual teachers to the rest of humanity, facilitating a massive spiritual awakening worldwide, mitigating many effects of the healing crisis that otherwise would have been far more severe and protracted.

A significant percentage of the population left the Earth plane though war and disease in the years following 2012. For a short time, cancer and heart disease rates rapidly increased in those unable to raise their consciousness, heal fears and process their unresolved karmas. The new consciousness was too much for them to assimilate and deal with, so for them karmic resolution came through a difficult passage from the Earth. Many of those involved in the old economic and political struc-

tures were part of this group of individuals. The global elite's reign of power collapsed soon after the 2012-2014 Iranian War leaving economic and political ruin worldwide, although the fatal wounds to the economy had already been inflicted long before then with the demise of the banking system and the fall-out from the Gulf of Mexico oil spill in 2010.

There were a few small scale wars as those losing power struggled in vain to maintain control, but they were swiftly brought to an end through the efforts of the enlightened ones and the Star Beings. The major Iranian War of 2012-2014 involving the US and Iran could not be stopped, for it was part of the healing process. However it was to be the last war, causing regional devastation in the Middle East and resulting in the loss of many human lives.

The Gulf of Mexico oil spill proved to be a total environmental disaster and the economic costs of the clear up and compensating those who lost income were so high it dealt a fatal blow to the US economy. It had been crippled with unsustainable levels of debt for many years, and when the oil disaster wiped out most of the US fisheries, rendering future drilling for oil in deep water too expensive and risky, it was too much for the US economy to bear and with the expense of the Iranian War the world's largest superpower finally fell to its knees . Its era of cheap oil had come to an end and chaos ensued as US suburbia built on the promise of endless cheap oil, ceased to function and millions of people endured extreme hardship as they suddenly found themselves out of work and unable to pay mortgages, having little option but to devote all their time to growing food.

Many US citizens, as well as people elsewhere lost their lives between 2012 and 2017 as starvation and hypothermia took its toll. Unfortunately for the US, preoccupied with fighting wars overseas, it had never invested in alternative technologies and the collapse of the oil based economy meant that even though there was still oil in the ground, there was no economic and corporate infrastructure remaining intact to remove it. Winters left people with no oil, gas or electricity to heat their homes and facing acute food shortages many perished.

The collapse of the US economy and the fallout from the Iranian War brought economic devastation worldwide and so other countries were unable to help, for they had their own issues to contend with. By the end of 2014 the global economy had totally collapsed, never to recover in the same form and the cities of the world had almost totally emptied out, for they were built not to nurture and sustain human beings, but were built simply as economic powerhouses. With no power for heating and lighting they became dark mausoleums and with the collapse of the food distribution networks, people left in mass.

By 2020 Nature had sensed the balance of power had changed, with trees and vigorous shrubs growing in the cracks of freeways, buildings and pavements. A few humans remained, surviving on canned and dried foods, but finding them was a challenge as most looting had already occurred. So for most of the time, an eerie silence was present in the cities, save for the occasional squawk of a crow or the smashing of a glass window pane falling loose from its fixings. It was not until 2025, some ten years after the emptying of the cities, that Nature had regained a strong enough foothold to support the return of wild animals and large numbers of birds. Any visitors to the cities now struggled to make it through the dense vegetation that had claimed almost every concrete surface and creeping plants were growing up the side of buildings, fatally weakening the structures and eventually bringing them down, though this process took over a century to complete. The steel skeletons of the largest skyscrapers loomed over the rapidly expanding forests around the cities for almost 250 years, standing testament to a past era.

The years from 2012 – 2017 saw most of the urban population migrate into the countryside and for those that survived the chaos of the economic collapse, growing food was the main preoccupation. Those that survived were those who were healthy, adaptable and fearless. For those who had not become free of fear, succumbed to psychological breakdown in the face of disorder and death and became unable to function. For them karmic resolution came through death and with their passage of suffering completed, these spirits ascended to the higher planes of love and light. Approximately 60% of the pre 2012 population survived the global economic collapse and the Iranian War. Apart from growing food, they devoted their lives to spirituality with the ascending spirits visibly recognising inner luminosity prior to their departure. This phenomenon brought great hope and showed there was a higher spiritual purpose to human existence and the possibility of liberation from suffering.

Humanity came together, finding common ground in spirituality and shared suffering. Many petty conflicts found resolution and strong vibrant communities quickly *developed outside of the old cities. For many people, spiritual enlightenment was rapid and by now the Star Beings were in open contact with the majority of the remaining humanity. They offered much in the way of spiritual assistance, healing and technological help to build new sustainable communities. Bio domes were built to fully harness the energies of the sun and to create new ecosystems that would eventually grow outside the confines of the domes, restocking nature with high vibrational plants and herbs that would heal the Earth on a deep level.*

The Star Beings brought to Earth new seeds that grew very healing foods as well as plants able to grow in and around toxic environments such as polluted lakes. The technologies and abilities of the Star Beings were able to raise the vibration of the soil, purify water and neutralise toxicity. They assisted the Earth with the purification process and within a few years, the food needs of humanity were met. For those communities who had completely restored their connection to nature and completed their healing, they were in want of nothing. They had every type of food imaginable and new ones too. The purification of the Earth brought about a renewed fertility in nature that modern day humanity had never seen. Fruits were large, tasty and abundant, nourishing the body deeply. No human had a need or the desire to kill an animal for its flesh. By 2025, hunger was eliminated. The purification and healing of the Earth had raised yields so high that there was surplus everywhere and there was ample land, for humanity had abandoned the eating of meat since so many carnivorous humans died in the healing crisis.

A collective grief due to the passing of so many people finally brought about a deep spiritual awakening and a full awareness of the consequences of past actions. The hardened heart of humanity was finally broken and in that space arose a deep love, sensitivity to nature and an intense sadness for all those lost in the transitions. Deep collective remorse arose for the damage done to the Earth, and many people underwent a very difficult emotional healing process. However the love of the Star Beings greatly assisted and accelerated the process. They were on hand to help whilst at the same time keeping a compassionate distance to allow the healing of humanity to occur. Some spirits continued to make the ascension out of matter showing the way for others to follow.

Humanity loved in a way it had never done before. The arising sensitivity and compassion was so powerful that no-one was left in need or in suffering. Nobody had an interest in economic activities, people simply shared what they had and everyone had enough. Greed was eliminated from the psyche of humanity, for many of those who had succumbed to greed had perished and those remaining learned deep lessons from the experience. The full healing of the heart of humanity took many years, but it had learned and matured. Those who died in the transitions were seen as teachers and guides to the rest of humanity. Every human who survived drew deep lessons from the experience, for almost everyone had lost someone close.

So the new humanity soon became strong and unity came from recognition of the spiritual light, with spiritual practice and ritual becoming an integral part of every individual life. Nature was respected and revered and the heart of humanity found deep and complete healing. By now nature had recovered and forest cover rapidly spread across the planet. The cities had become a combination of an open air museum and a safari park, with many simply impenetrable. Nature had done well in taking back what was rightfully hers.

Though the new humanity lived in total harmony with nature, they also had a wide array of technologies to assist them. New materials were discovered with the help of the Star Beings that enabled the construction of eco-buildings and the utilisation of solar power energy on a large scale. Under the supervision of the Star Beings, the nuclear weapon stockpiles of the planet were rendered harmless and all toxic nuclear wastes were teleported into the centre of the Sun for disposal. The nuclear power stations were closed down, for humanity discovered various means of generating infinite energy out of the ether itself. These technologies, suppressed and kept from humanity by the old elite system now became quickly accessible to all of humanity.

The Star Beings brought technologies that rendered conventional transportation redundant. Teleportation became widespread, in an instant anyone could go any-where on the Earth and with advanced portal technology, those of a high enough vibration were able to visit the stars directly without the need for star-craft. Star-craft however became useful for mining asteroids or for inter planetary missions. Almost any human being now had the means to take a trip to any planet in the Solar Sys-tem, such trips became commonplace and the physical exploration of space accelerated. Many chose to remain on Earth, but a sizeable sector of humanity opted to set up colonies elsewhere in the Solar System and beyond.

Peace was restored on the Earth and by 2025 the healing processes had been completed. Approximately one billion humans had ascended through vibratory ascension and were now immortals living elsewhere in higher dimensional solar systems. Around two billion lost their lives in the transitions through war or disease and three billion remained to form a new humanity – based on love, peace and common understanding. This new humanity had a deep and intimate relationship with nature and no-one thought of doing, or did anything that would harm any other living being. Every human heart knew love and demonstrated it through action and deed, so humanity became an enlightened race purified of greed, hatred and ignorance - long known as the three poisons.

Hospitals lay empty and abandoned for everyone enjoyed perfect health. Life was an expression of connection to Divinity and all beings joyfully celebrated their spiritual connection to Source whilst always having the deepest respect for the Earth. Natural abundance prospered and life spans increased dramatically. Death became very rare and often people instead opted for conscious ascension to higher planes after a long and healthy life in service to the rest of humanity. Humanity enjoyed an open relationship with the Star Beings and the arrival of them had undoubtedly played a massive part in lifting humanity out of suffering and ignorance.

The Star Beings cannot visit humanity openly now, for our collective vibration is not high enough for most of us to see them and if we could somehow see them it would generate too much fear and be counterproductive. It is likely that the governments of the world have been in contact with some Extra-Terrestrials, but they are likely to be other three-dimensional species and though they may have things to teach humanity, they will not be the ones that bring the deepest transformation and healing to us. It is likely that any species in contact with the world's governments will not have purely altruistic agendas for humanity and discernment will be required if or when these beings are introduced to us. They may well have technologies that can help humanity out of its current predicament but they may also have an ulterior motive for sharing the technology.

The Star Beings from higher dimensions, who have the interests of humanity at heart, are visiting spiritually receptive individuals who are working for the healing of humanity. Anyone in contact with the higher dimensional beings will be working to raise the consciousness of humanity to the level where more individuals will be able to see them. The agendas of the Star Beings are to empower individuals to help heal humanity and to reduce the collective fear of Higher Beings and to prepare the collective of humanity for open contact, which requires a shift in conscious vibration toward the spiritual planes. Then they can appear to us in mass, but they will not come in spacecraft made from matter, rather they will appear as translucent rainbow beings or in light ships and will have the ability to appear out of thin air. They will have their own technologies in the higher dimensions, but physical craft will not be required for them to appear on Earth.

The Star Beings will help humanity make the final passage and bring an end to the rule of the elite, who for decades have suppressed and prevented the progression of humanity. Their rule has enslaved humanity to a system built on false beliefs, lies and a separation from love – and has used fear tactics to threaten anyone challenging those beliefs with ridicule, intimidation and in some cases murder. However the consciousness of humanity has finally raised enough to bring about a shift in the balance of power. The elite are now very weak and mortally wounded. Knowing their games, lies and illusions are beginning to be exposed, they will resort to more desperate measures to maintain their control.

This desperation is now obvious and many people are awakening to the realisation that the governments simply cannot be trusted, nor do they have the ability to exercise moral leadership and act in the best interests for humanity. It is not too late for them to admit their mistakes, come clean and to make better choices. However as they are in a state of fear and denial, they will unlikely to be able to do so and thus their power will diminish. They will have to step down or be peacefully ousted out by the common people.

The end of the elite and their associated systems will bring about a transformation and liberation far beyond that which most people are able to fully comprehend as most of humanity is still enslaved to conditionings and beliefs that are keeping them in fear. Fear keeps individuals separated from a realisation of their true spiritual nature and the ability to live a life in love, free from ill-health and suffering. The elite has done nothing to prevent the widespread contamination of our environment, food and water with heavy duty toxins which dull our minds and senses, robbing us of our ability to see and think clearly.

The final purification of our bodies and our hearts along with the end of the elite will bring about an age of utopia where everyone will have everything they need, spiritual knowledge will be widespread and truth will prevail. This new age will be free of the institutions that have controlled humanity for so long, the power will be in the hands and hearts of the common people. The ability to determine our destiny will be returned to us. With our intuition and mental faculties fully restored along with the re-awakening of love in the heart of humanity, we will make the right choices. We will become a spiritually advanced, wise and loving race with the help of the Star Beings, and our long term future on Earth and elsewhere in the galaxy will be assured.

Chapter 12

The star gates open – Receiving the Rainbow Key

At the time of writing it is summer 2010 and the higher dimensional portals (star gates) on the Earth are beginning to open. Where the leylines of the Earth meet, energetic vortices exist and these energetic hubs act as portals to other dimensions. As discussed earlier in the book, the Earth and Galactic Core line up only once every 26,000 years. However in the period of alignment which is approximately ten years, the leyline grid of the planet becomes supercharged with multidimensional energies enabling hidden portals and star gates to become active. Some of these portals are naturally occurring vortices, however in other locations benevolent extra-terrestrials acting as the guardians of humanity have constructed star gates to allow passage between the different dimensions. Where a star gate has been built over a natural portal, passage is possible to different star systems and visitors from elsewhere can come to Earth.

The star gates allow passage of higher dimensional craft into the Earth's biosphere. After spending some time on Knapp Hill in Wiltshire (UK), one night - a star gate site, I soon saw several unidentified flying craft simply appearing and disappearing out of clear cloudless thin air! These crafts sometimes manifested as coloured or golden orbs, sometimes with haloes and would race across the sky at incredible speed, change direction abruptly and sometimes change form or explode into a burst of light, akin to fireworks. The full opening of the star gates will bring about all kinds of phenomena that humanity currently has no experience of and so we will be called to be open-minded and expand our consciousness as our expected limitations and exclusions of ordinary reality become transcended before our eyes.

Conventional science has confined such events to the realm of the paranormal or even labelled them as hallucinations, however humanity will soon be incorporating these phenomena into everyday reality as more orbs, crafts and other higher dimensional objects emerge from these star gates. We do not need to fear, as these phenomena are the work of loving higher intelligences, coming to Earth to bring about transformation and healing. The more open minded we can be to what is possible, the more our consciousness will expand and be able to integrate the new possibilities.

As these energy vortices and star gates become supercharged, which is now in progress, they bring powerful healing energies to this planet and if we are receptive we can receive massive healing by visiting these sites. Sometimes the vibrations emanating from these sites can be very intense, but they have a purpose to raise the vibration of our bodies, bringing impurities to the surface for purification and release. All kinds of experiences can be had by visiting the star gate sites and recently I have undergone a profound transformation in consciousness, which brought through further communications as the following writings from my log illustrate;-

Visiting the Knapp Hill star gate last night brought about a change in awareness. When I arrived there late in the evening, immediately I became aware of an influx of higher dimensional communication. It was as if mind and heart were receiving telepathic messages and they were perceived in the heart as a flood of new emotions and incredible feelings of love. In the mind they were perceived as coloured rays and infusions into the conscious awareness.

My aura became extremely energized and I was able to feel vibrations pouring into my being from interstellar space, bringing about a deeper awakening of Star-seed consciousness and a deeper experience of love from the Star Beings. A beautiful angelic face from another world appeared in my consciousness, transparent but yet incredibly colourful and from its heart came a multitude of healing rays that filtered through all levels of my being, rejuvenating, awakening, stirring, healing, opening and purifying. The being rose a hand and the palm became a pulsing star of shining light and it communicated this was the light for healing humanity. It channelled it into my being and I felt very humbled in the experience of this loving contact. Freed of any fear of them, I was able to simply receive this love and this love spoke the ancient wisdom of these enlightened intelligences - this love heals everything when there is no fear. This love is also a guide as the experience left me with a deeper clarity.

The rainbow being communicated that this love was still far from a full expression, that maybe only years of contact can fully bring about.

"This love knows and sees all of you, that is why many people are afraid of us, because they cannot hide from their wounds and control dramas. Contact with us requires them to heal those aspects of themselves in fear and suffering. Only in a state of total truth to oneself, free of illusion and misconception, can one have a deep relationship with us. We come to visit you when your heart is deeply purified and all your fears are gone. In these

spaces you can perceive us through your enhanced awareness and perception and benefit from our communication. Your world will soon enter a healing crisis and we come to assist the Earthly helpers with this transition in humanity. If you hear our messages, then you have a role to play with the healing of humanity."

The final communication from them at that time went on to say that the star gates on the Earth are now opening and the higher dimensional energies are pouring into our Solar System.

"A wave of higher energy so massive and profound is about to enter the life of every human being. It comes not from us, but from the centre of your Galaxy and funnels through the portals. It restores and heals the Earth and nothing or no-one can stop it. The governments of your world are deeply afraid and want to control the star gates, but know that their efforts are futile. No weapons can destroy or interfere with the star gates and this purification and healing will continue.

The Earth is fully awakening to its higher dimensional nature and for all of you open to this healing this spells the beginning of your full enlightenment and transformation. Love the Earth now, and it will carry you through the transitions, it will hold you and nourish you and all of natures gifts will be bestowed onto you at the end of the purification cycle. Have no fear and trust that we and the Earth will guide you. For those that do not wish to love the Earth will soon be leaving, as their lives draw to a difficult close. Again we reiterate - have compassion for these people but do not let them draw you into their stories of suffering."

The Wiltshire Knapp Hill star gate is a very energetic point on the Earth and can powerfully transform the consciousness of any being upon it. So as well as being portals for the Star Beings, orbs and other light-ships, they are portals that are emitting powerful healing energies that have an effect on the individual and the planet as a whole. These energies are being transmitted along the leylines of the Earth resulting in an increase in the Earths vibration and initiating purification processes, including increases in earthquakes and extreme weather events. Channelling the healing vibrations into our own being, cleansing the heart and the pineal gland, they also bring about purification processes in us, so we may fully integrate these energies and become a conscious multidimensional being.

As well as the Wiltshire star gate, I believe the Egyptian pyramid complex is another example of a star gate to a star in the constellation of Orion. The whole complex viewed from above clearly shows a representation of the Orion constellation, with the three main pyramids representing the three stars of Orion's belt. The builders of the pyramids who appear to have more advanced technologies than we have today, suggesting the possibility of them not being human. They seem to have harnessed the power of the natural leyline vortex beneath the site of the pyramids to accomplish interstellar travel.

It is unlikely the Egyptians would have gone to so much effort to create a burial chamber for a great king. The amount of stone in the pyramid is phenomenal, as is the mathematical precision in the layout and stacking of the stones. On my visit to the pyramids, many shafts depicted in the history books for some reason have been mysteriously cemented up and the deeper recesses of the pyramids are sealed - inaccessible to the public and under armed guard. The behaviour of the Egyptian authorities today appears to point toward the hiding of something. Personally I felt a very strong higher dimensional vibration emanating from the depths of the pyramids when I was inside, not something I experienced inside other pharaohs tombs in Egypt.

As 2012 approaches we may see the energies intensifying around the pyramids of Giza, and sometime in 2012 we can expect to meet the next wave of visitors as the star gate becomes functional again. I say the next wave, as it is likely the pyramids were used during Earths history regularly as an entry/exit point into higher dimensions and the pyramids are likely to be much older than they are claimed to be. If one looks carefully at paintings in Egyptian tombs, one can find paintings of extra-terrestrials, beings in flying machines and humanoids with features such as elongated heads which are not supported by the fossil records on Earth. This suggests these beings are the Star Beings rather than residents of Earth. The star gates can only operate in times of Galactic alignment and hence visitation of Earth by higher dimensional extra-terrestrials is sporadic, occurring at times of Galactic cycle completion. This 26,000 year period is long enough for the culture of humanity to forget about any past Star Being contact and influence, and descend into a state of consciousness closed to the idea of their existence.

Star gate travel would not have been as simple as just entering the pyramid or other portal. It is also required to have a vibration high enough to enter the star gate. This requires ones aura to be purified and sufficiently cleared of emotional and physical blockages to facilitate the transmutation and teleportation process. With a high enough vibration, the physicality of the body can be temporarily transcended, with the blueprint of the light body being responsible for disassembly and reassembly of the physical atoms of the body during the teleportation process. Without a sufficiently awakened and evolved light body, this process is impossible and someone walking into a star gate with a low vibration will experience nothing.

Someone of a high enough vibration entering into the star gate would have the experience of entering a spiralling rainbow tunnel of light and then emerging into the fifth dimensional realm of light beyond the physical plane. Everything would be sparkling and there would be rainbow light emanating from the ethers. Here one would meet the Star Beings, see the light-ships, the orbs, the light cities – for here is the source of the light and higher intelligence now beginning to filter through the star gates. By the time the star gates close, the Earth will have been totally transformed into a higher dimensional state and restored to its original pristine condition, carrying the new humanity, with the controlling forces gone and the light workers having left the Earth through the portals for other dimensional worlds.

Being able to reach star gate vibration is thus now an important part in the evolution of an individual, for if we can do so, we will be able to make the transition into higher dimensional consciousness and avoid the suffering in the final healing crisis. Making star gate vibration is a sign that our healing and karmic purification is almost over, and that we have reached a vibration compatible for being a part of the new humanity or having the opportunity for higher dimensional ascension to worlds closer to the Galactic Core.

Attaining the necessary vibration results in one receiving what I call the Rainbow Key. The Rainbow Key is what enables one to access the portals and star gates and is given to us by the wise Star Beings when we reach a certain level of vibratory evolution. To reach this point requires a massive purging of negative emotional baggage and physical toxicity, which creates the clarity of mind to perceive the higher vibrations and to understand what is being seen without succumbing to fear. The purging process also clears the chakras, enabling them to handle the intense energies of the portals. The Rainbow Key is an auric enhancement, and being granted to us by the Star Beings, prevents misuse of the portals or the possible bodily disintegration that would occur if lower vibratory beings were able to enter the portals without the necessary purification.

In this way, the star gates are totally impenetrable to those carrying fear and hatred, preventing those with harmful agendas crossing over into the light realms. Hence this is why the governments are so afraid of the opening of the star gates, because they wish to control their opening and what comes through, however both are impossible. At this moment in time, a star gate is about to open in the Aden Gulf and a flotilla of warships is just off the coast of Yemen. However none of these warships will be able to effect any change on the star gate, none of the military will be able to enter, and all they can do is stand by and do nothing. Entry is solely granted by the Star Beings on completion of the purification passage. Only those with pure hearts and minds will be able to visit the worlds beyond. Receiving the rainbow key into these dimensions results in a sudden shift of consciousness along with an ability to perceive and interact with other dimensions whilst operating in the Earth plane.

One experience of communication with the Star Beings gave more insights into the role of star gates for facilitating teleportation, inter-dimensional travel and departure from the Earth by passage through the Suns core for those individuals who are karmically eligible for this kind of ascension.

"When the star gates open , if you are free from fear and pure in heart, you will be able to freely come and go from this dimension and walk into luminous realms where we have light ships, cities and portals to other parts of the galaxy, where many beautiful worlds exist circling multiple suns. All beings here embrace love and immortality. For those with the Rainbow Key, all these worlds are open to you to visit and for some of you they will be your new residence once your spiritual work on Earth becomes completed.

The star gates allow our light ships from our dimension to visit your world on the completion of the Galactic alignment. Some of you have chosen to exit the Earth through the process of immortal ascension and so your lives have been a purification and preparation process so you are able to reach the vibration required to be able to use the star gates. If you can perceive now the opening of the star gates it is likely you will be able to leave the

Earth in one of our light crafts when your service to humanity is completed. The raising of your vibration will enable the denser parts of your being to fall away, which if not released would be an impediment to star gate travel, for the energies at the centre of the Sun are so intense that conscious passage would be impossible without the purification and healing. This is why not all of you can leave the Earth – only those healed enough to be able to journey into the Sun's core can leave. However many others of you will soon be able to explore other regions of three dimensional space through more conventional crafts once the technologies filter through into your consciousness after the purification and healing crisis has been completed around 2025."

The beings explained again how star gates work, by utilising the natural energies of the leylines and creating a tunnel into other dimensions. Many of the star gates are energetically connected to and powered by the Suns energies and hence using the star gates to shift dimension requires a passage through the Suns core. They explained how each human being had the latent ability to attain star gate vibration and this can become manifest after a period of purification and healing. When this ability awakens, one can use the star gates even if one is some distance away, for one can use the nearest leyline to travel along the leyline matrix and access the star gate. When you wish to make a journey, a funnel will open up in your chakra system and your whole being will temporarily dissolve into it and emerge elsewhere. This will also enable site to site teleportation on Earth for those with a sufficient vibration.

They explained that in the higher dimensional planetary systems, Galactic Core alignment is continuous, for these worlds have orbits that do not depart from the Galactic plane. On these worlds, the star gates are functional all of the time and thus the level of spiritual development amongst intelligences in these spheres is much more advanced, being free of physical bodies and constantly in alignment with the Galactic Core vibrations.

All planets have an energetic matrix (a leyline system), allowing higher dimensional energies to flow through the planets interior raising the overall vibration of the planetary sphere in question. It is these planetary matrices that allow the formation of vortices and enable transport in and out of other dimensions. If we can heal ourselves enough, we can become attuned to these energies and begin to develop an understanding of portal mechanics which will allow humanity to transcend current transportation limitations. The new humanity stands to utilise these powerful natural energies to achieve clean, free and swift transportation anywhere on the planet as well as elsewhere in the Galaxy.

Any civilisation that can raise their consciousness to this kind of level has the opportunity for full healing, open contact with the Star Beings and a utopian society where technologies based on the energies of the light dimensions provide limitless clean energy, bringing about an end to dependence on finite energy sources such as oil. This switch to free energy will be a crucial factor in the development of the new humanity. For that to happen, the dynamics that have led to the elite suppressing such technologies from humanity so as to enslave humanity to dependence on oil, will need to be resolved and healed. It is likely the unfolding of the Gulf of Mexico oil spill will expose all these issues and present us with an opportunity to grow and learn. Oil will not be a part of the new humanity.

Chapter 13

A Roadmap for Healing

For many of us the experience of communicating with Star Beings and entering portals into different dimensions is not an everyday experience. So for those who wish to experience these dimensions of consciousness and experience the deep healing from the loving higher intelligences, this chapter is intended as a roadmap for healing.

Becoming free of suffering and fully integrating higher dimensional consciousness comes about after a long period of healing work on all aspects of our being, physical, emotional and spiritual. For those living conventional lifestyles, the healing process will call for us to reject long standing beliefs and ideas that we have held to for many years. This process in itself can bring up a lot of fear, for if we are to reject convention for something else we cannot yet experience, it seems like a leap of faith into the unknown. The healing process calls for us to trust that as we reject those things that no longer serve humanity we will be presented with new opportunities. Many times in my life I have surrendered to change and have lost the fear of doing that, in return I have always been rewarded spiritually. Whenever the path has called for me to leave a job or other situation that no longer serves, after making the conscious decision and stepping out into the unknown, the universe has always responded to my intention by providing more fortuitous circumstances for spiritual growth.

The challenge we face now is to trust our intuition, which comes from within, rather than trusting the external messages we see around us. Part of our healing is to recognise that the world leaders cannot help us and we cannot look to them to solve our problems. Often we look externally for guidance – either from the leadership, or to religions. However the deepest wisdom is contained within our being, there is nothing outside of ourselves that can help us and all we need is within. So the healing journey calls for us to tune in to our own intuition and discover the healing spiritual messages that can come through from the higher dimensions to guide and heal us. When we lose the fear of trusting our inner voice it becomes strong, we can receive an abundance of inner wisdom and guidance and then we will begin to experience the process of the inner unfolding of the spiritual world. This then awakens our heart and brings about an inner empowerment and confidence. Once the heart is open, this fuels our spiritual development.

A good starting point for most people on the way to healing is to forge this inner connection with the intuition and this can be done through meditation, spiritual practice and the stilling of the mind. Looking to ones dreams can also awaken the inner wisdom. Any kind of spiritual practice that awakens your heart, stills your mind, and gives you a humanitarian (rather than economic) perspective on the global situation today is worth taking up.

Healing the inner child is also a vital part of our transformation and any childhood issues that remain unresolved will be an impediment to healing. By facing ourselves and our wounds with awareness and love, we give ourselves the opportunity to heal them. At some point in our lives, we will find ourselves in an intense and painful passage, but this should be viewed as beneficial and one should never try and shirk away from it and hide in emotionally comfortable activities such as drinking alcohol or overeating, for if we do we prevent the healing process from completing itself. The more courage we can find to endure the passages, the greater reward one receives and we will find our emotional capacity will expand making further healing easier.

The healing process ultimately will need to become our life work if we are to make the most spiritual progress, as for many of us there will be a lot of transformation and change to bring about. We do not need to renounce our responsibilities, but it is important to create spaces in our lives for our healing and spirituality and if our current situation does not allow that, then we may need to make some life changes. Time in nature is deeply beneficial as well as healing and for anyone living an urban lifestyle, I would advise considering a change to a more rural existence in tune with the cycles and beauty of nature.

Paying attention to ethics will help us deeply and helps us to achieve karmic purification. Looking at where we have hurt others and making amends is a very valuable part of the healing journey, as well as giving us the sensitivity of heart and emotional fortitude to undergo the more difficult spiritual work – the conquering of all fear. As explained earlier in the book, fear is a major impediment and only through healing our fears of death and non-human intelligences can we experience the higher dimensions fully.

In the end, what we ideally would want to aspire to is nothing short of a full core healing where all obscurations, confusions, fears and physical blockages are relinquished. Then we can experience spiritual rebirth into a new reality of love, light, abundance, joy and physical wellbeing free from any illness. The following channelled communication from the Higher Beings came after a long period of spiritual work and healing. It also came a day or two before giving a talk on the roadmap to healing, so I will share it here, in the hope it inspires readers to find deeper healing, meaning to their lives and the joy of meeting the Higher Beings.

"I am a messenger from a 9th dimensional blue star system in the Ra Stellar Cluster and come to communicate the messages that will ultimately facilitate the full core healings for your species if you are open to the possibility. My communication is an offering and no-one is obliged to follow any religion or do anything if they choose not to. All have freewill - such is the Law of the Universe.

Many years ago in your time, the elders of our collectives saw forward in time and could see that humanity was approaching a time of planetary crisis. It was agreed that spirits from Ra and other Star Systems would incarnate in human form in this time, channelling the wisdom and communications that would help humanity make it through the transitions ahead on your planet. Hence some of you will now be awakening to the truth that you originated from another world and have opted to come here to help the rest of humanity.

On the Ra home-world, more appropriately called a nexus or portal hub - we live outside of time and conventional space and are immortal light beings. We are free from suffering, disease and all afflictions caused by separation from the Divine Source. Existing on a finer energetic dimension, we are invisible to humans until you reach a certain degree of vibratory healing, after which you can receive our communications and enter into a relationship with us. We love you, as we do all of the different aspects of creation and ultimately we desire for you to complete your healings, so you can make the ascension into our reality and enjoy an existence amongst the stars.

A complete core healing is possible which enables you to transform your energetic vibration and consciousness to a point where you transcend all sufferings, recognise and experience the universal vibrations of love and are able to perceive and integrate multidimensional consciousness. At the end of your healing journey, there is the potential for you to experience a profound and deeply divine love that currently most of you are unable to receive because of the obscurations and blockages in your hearts.

The starting point for your healing is to work with your body and cleanse it of all toxins. The food you eat is very important, and only the purest foods direct from nature will bring about the deepest level of healing. Eating the creatures of the Earth is one of the first transitions to make, for whilst you are involved in the unnecessary suffering of animals, your heart will be unable to experience the deeper sensitivity required for the full core healings. It also poisons and clogs up your body, causing most of the disease so widespread on your planet.

The colon wall will accumulate all manner of physical and emotional toxins if your diet is not pure, dampening your vibration and robbing you of vitality. These toxins must be released if you are to embody and integrate the higher consciousness. If you are resistant to eating a purer diet, it will be because an accumulation of emotional toxins have created negative attachments to eating certain kinds of harmful foods. These attachments need to be recognised, resolved and released with a loving awareness of one's own body. The negative projections toward vegans and vegetarians by the meat eaters on your world are an outward sign of this accumulation of emotional toxins in the colonic wall. Loving one's body and treating it well is a big step on the road to healing.

Understand that the leadership of your world, themselves carrying toxins in their bodies, thus do not have the sensitivity and depth of heart required to bring forth the changes that are required in humanity. Carrying toxins, they do not recognise that toxicity is even a problem and this situation has become problematic to a point where the water supply of most of humanity is poisoned with heavy metals, pesticides and harmful chemicals which weaken your immune system, cause neurological damage and suppress higher spiritual function. At the same time, the pharmaceutical industries on your planet, profiteering in sickness, continue to distribute chemically toxic 'medicines' that have all manner of negative effects on the physical and emotional body.

It is vital for those of you wishing the deepest healings to move away from pharmaceuticals and to avoid drinking the tap water at all costs. Only drink from springs or the cleanest rivers. A few microbes in natural water are nothing compared to the chemical cocktail in processed water and your body will adapt to become immune to *these organisms, enabling you to drink from a wider range of rivers and streams with no ill effect.*

The fluoride present in tap water weakens your teeth and bones, often necessitating the placing of metallic mercury dental fillings - another toxin that must be avoided at all costs. The vaccinations promoted and encouraged by your current health systems all contain toxic levels of mercury. The health systems of your planet cannot offer you healing for they have been formulated and created by groups of people who have not healed themselves on a core level. Thus they do not recognise the true cause of disease and can offer little in the way of lasting healing for many ailments. Almost every disease on your planet is caused by an accumulation of toxins and can be healed through a pure diet, the intake of pure water and engaging in a deep cleansing of the heart.

Understand that the sweets and drinks that most of you enjoyed as a child contain toxic preservatives and sugars that have long term negative effects on one's health. Hold no animosity toward your families, for they simply did not know and move away from eating them. Jellies are made from crushed up animal bones and muscles from the slaughterhouses and white sugar is made clean by sieving it through charcoaled cattle bones. Fruit squashes are nothing more than watered down chemical cocktails. Most of your toothpastes contain fluoride, which along with sugar intake causes tooth decay and the seepage of harmful bacteria into the body. Fluoride does not prevent tooth decay – volcanic ash containing fluoride is responsible for the dental and skeletal weakening of Icelandic livestock, and fluoride affects humans in the same way as well as acting as a pineal toxin.

When your body is in perfect health and free of physical toxins, one is able to attain a deeper degree of heart healing. Ones emotional heart cannot open fully and receive healing, if the physical heart is clogged with the debris from poor eating. The physical burden of toxins creates energetic blockages that are a factor in the manifestation of anger, resentment, fear and violence.

Heart healing requires you to transform any impediment that prevents you from developing a deeper sensitivity to nature and love for others. Toxic overloads on the body have contributed to the closing down of your heart chakra, blunting your ability to feel on a deep level and preventing you from experiencing healing, loving vibrations. Thus the healing of the body and heart are intimately connected, both aspects must be brought to a level of full healing if you are to receive the deepest illuminations and ultimately transcend the human condition.

Surrender to love, for love heals all discomforts and afflictions of the human heart. By closing to love, you deny yourselves the healing you so deeply yearn for. Never fear love for it can never harm you. Love opens you up, and restores your vibration to one of harmony and peace as fear based tensions are released.

All fears must be confronted and released, for they drain vitality and whilst unacknowledged they are a subconscious menace, leading you to act from places of confusion and animosity, creating for yourselves further negative karmic consequences. The fear of death, leads you to over indulge in physical enjoyments to compensate and mask the deep existential inner crisis. Healing this crisis brings about deep transformation. Work with the dying and sick people on your planet and by doing so it is possible to experience compassion and an opening of the heart, which then leaves no place for fear to reside. Your collective fear of death has lowered your vibration to the point where you are unable to perceive realities beyond the physical plane which has then compounded the fear.

Healing the fear of death will result in a massive vibratory boost and along with an open heart and clean body, will enable you to experience spiritual rebirth in higher dimensional consciousness which will enable you to consciously perceive the afterlife. Having a direct experience of non-physical reality will deepen your understanding, and begin to facilitate your enlightenment. This is the minimum level of healing ideally that you would want to attain in your lifetime. If you are unable to perceive beyond the physical and understand the higher realities before death, the death process can bring up a lot of fear.

So once you have healed your body, opened your heart on a very deep level and had some perception of the non-physical dimensions, you will then develop the awareness that there are other dimensions of existence beyond the Earthly plane and that there is the possibility of immortality and ascension out of matter-existence. The final and largest impediment to the ascension is ones karmic accumulations.

Karmic healing is required to make the ascension. Fully healed vibratory beings do not inhabit the third dimensional reality, and so your existence in your realities ultimately is an opportunity to heal and release your vibratory defilements and blockages, so you may ascend into the immortal realms of consciousness. Healing karma is made possible by engaging with the heart and holistic healing. With a purity of heart, mind and body, you will have developed a deeper sensitivity and by doing so will recognise the causes of all your suffering. Having done this, you will be able to act in different ways, preventing further karmic accumulations and enabling the transformation of existing ones. Karma can be healed through firstly becoming aware of it and then sending light and love into the corresponding body or heart blockage, whilst allowing yourself to experience the difficult emotions associated with the karma so they can be released. Finally cultivate love and forgiveness towards yourself and aspire to act in more conscious and loving ways in future.

Having communicated the above, it is a very difficult and arduous journey. Yet with an open heart and a determined spirit one can complete this healing journey. It is a prerequisite for the long term survival for humanity, for as many of you as possible to undertake this complete vibratory healing. This is because in the process, all human conflicts are recognised as operating from places of fear and misunderstanding and the full healings bring the wisdom to see the cause behind any difficulty. As you come toward the end of your transformative healings, you will receive in your heart such a deeply powerful yet gentle cosmic love, that any remaining healings are swift as the final obscurations are melted away.

Then in your being comes forth the Luminous Consciousness. You may have the experience of the arising within your heart of a white luminous star, and the visitation of angels, star beings and nature spirits. They come to acknowledge and honour you as you reach this place and they come with energetic healings to raise yet further your level of vibration. This place is the end of the human journey, for all suffering is transcended and the inner luminosity if deeply recognised and embodied, will burn away all karmic defilements rendering further human existence unnecessary.

In this consciousness, undoubtedly you will be able to receive our communications and realise that you are not alone in the Universe. Having purified and cleansed your being and having transcended fear, you are able to receive our love and wisdom. Never again will you feel unloved or separated from the eternal bliss of the light consciousness. Our communications from the higher dimensions bring about your full healings, for we have deep love for you and wish your species to make it through the transition into enlightened awareness with the minimum of suffering.

A future awaits you – the full immensity and magnitude of it beyond human comprehension. Once this light awareness is recognised by most of humanity, it will bring about such a deep and divine transformation that nothing of your old world will remain. This is the purpose of the Earth changes - to bring about this new consciousness. This consciousness will ultimately bring all of humanity back into alignment with the cosmic vibrations. Then you will meet us - immortal star beings from higher planes, having completed the vibratory healing you will be able to perceive us and receive our love.

When you complete your healing, you will have come to the end of your human journey. Know that your continued existence on Earth is then only to help others reach this level of healing. The human condition once understood, is then transcended. You achieve graduation of consciousness and earn the ability to leave the human condition along with all suffering. Then you will realise that the reality of a human being is that of a Star Being that has fallen into unconsciousness and forgotten its nature. You will realise you are one of us too and joyfully you will reconnect with your awareness of interstellar immortality. Before you leave your Earth and come back to our loving realm there is one further mission for you. It is asked that you render your whole life in service to the Higher Love and to the restoration of peace, for the Earth must be healed and restored before one can leave. It is an act of honouring the planetary entity which has supported you for so long. In this honouring of the Earth, you are energetically and karmically released, your work on Earth is done, your suffering and pain is over and you are restored and remade in the blueprint of the highest dimensions of light..

Know that the embodiment of this consciousness will ultimately restore humanity to a state of perfect love and enlightenment. Every problem on your planet will be healed and your civilisation will enter into the deepest and most loving divine celebration ever known in the history of humanity, as you all recognise your deeper nature, turn to one another in peace, love and joy and engage with the work of healing your planet."

Being receptive to the possibility of the above healings requires us to have an open heart and mind, inviting us to think outside of the box, and to move beyond convention. The conventional mindset may keep us in a comfort zone as it does not rock our emotional boat, but it prevents us from growing. Often we remain attached to old ideals and beliefs because of fear, but if we do not challenge ourselves to grow we can become stuck in the old consciousness. If we do not make progress in transforming our consciousness and ways of life, the collapse of the old systems will be very traumatic for us. That stress, trauma and suffering is avoidable through becoming open to spiritual possibilities now. By voluntarily choosing the path of change and transformation we draw into our lives joy, abundance, guidance and spiritual illumination.

Recently I went to a conventional social party, and the reality of the old consciousness was brought home to me, and having moved out of this mindset many years prior, it was a challenge to remain in the hall for there was a massive rift in vibration and there was little common ground. The party was held in a village hall and there were tables of food laid out. There was nothing organic to be found anywhere. People were having a good time by drinking alcohol, eating sausages on sticks and grapes covered in visible pesticides. Whilst music was playing in the background people were gorging themselves with huge pieces of cream cakes laden with sugar and drinking fizzy drinks containing toxic aspartame.

Some of the guests were showing visible signs of toxic overload on the body and yet for these people this was one of the highlights of their lives. I felt like an alien visitor, carrying my own spring water and eating an organic salad with sprouting seeds, sitting on the sidelines working out how I could possibly interact with these people. Any attempt to do so felt false and whatever I could say about my life was so far beyond their ordinary parameters of thinking and belief it immediately challenged them and made them feel uncomfortable.

For people in traditional and conventional ways of thinking, it is time to consider alternatives. The alternatives are often viewed as oddballs, cranks or even insane by some conventional people, yet it is the alternative consciousness that carries the solutions to the global problems that conventional living has generated. If we are to receive healing and deep understanding on spiritual matters, embracing the alternative is a vital step. Ultimately all of conventional thinking and ways of doing things will have to be renounced across the board if we are to save our planet and survive as a species. The deepest healing and illumination comes from rejecting almost everything we have been brought up to believe and have been taught by the conventional institutions. This does not mean we should be unthankful for our upbringing, as often our parents only knew the conventional way, and only by experiencing years of conventional life and finding its limitations do we finally make some spiritual ground and open up to wider possibilities.

The older generations may well find it very difficult to embrace or understand the new consciousness, so we need to be compassionate towards them, whilst trying to find ways to communicate our knowledge and insights so they can come to a deeper understanding. For those who are departing this world through death, who have little understanding, we can still show compassion toward them so their passage is as comfortable as possible. It is likely the increase in planetary vibration will cause a sharp increase in the number of elderly deaths, for many of these people will not have the ability to assimilate the new consciousness, nor the physical strength to withstand the detoxification required to heal the body and cleanse the pineal gland. The deaths of these individuals will be another opportunity for the rest of humanity to be compassionate and the act of being compassionate is a very powerful healer of fear, so contributing to the overall healing of the collective.

Another aspect of our healing, I have not yet written about but which is also important is the renunciation of cultural programming. The world around us contains many hidden messages including many on a subliminal level, designed to keep us unaware of the bigger picture. The vast amount of advertising everywhere often plays on our vulnerabilities and desires, and creates the illusion that the material world can bring fulfilment, happiness and satisfaction. The media, constantly reporting negative stories, play on our fears and keep us in a state of paralysis, not knowing how to act in the face of such overwhelming global pessimism. Rarely do the news broadcasts carry any stories of inspiration, hope or healing. I believe the media is censored and the content tailored so as to present an inaccurate portrayal of what is really going on and any vital information, such as the true extent of the Gulf of Mexico oil spill, or of UFO visitations, are screened out so the general public do not receive information that would be vital for our awakening and enlightenment.

Thus we have to use our own discernment and not take anything we are told at face value. It is important to understand that we are being programmed on many levels by the elite, media and corporations to embrace a culture which is ultimately based on a lie and enslaves us to the economic machine, offering no spiritual fulfilment or answers to any of the global problems facing us today. The healing of humanity will come about when more of us are able to see through the fictions of cultural programming and develop the fearlessness to reject social and conventional conditionings that have done nothing other than to keep us in a space of fear. It is these conditionings and the programming through media and advertising that are used by the global elite and the corporate industry to control our thoughts and our minds. We are then imprisoned in a reality where we are separated from our hearts and driven by fear.

If we can heal our own fears, then this cultural programming ceases to have any power over us and we become liberated, and at the same time the power the elite has over us is weakened. Being able to see through the lies and distortions of Western culture, we are able to see it offers no promise or hope of a sustainable civilisation built on love, harmony and peace. When we see and understand the illusion, we are free. The Western economic culture can be seen as a huge machine slowly but surely moving toward an abyss. Each one of us is a cog in the machine and when we awaken we become like a cog spinning in the opposite direction or a spanner in the works.

If a large percentage of us can awaken, the machine will malfunction and stop before plunging into the abyss, reducing the human suffering associated with the collapse. The sooner this out of control machine is stopped, the less chaos and suffering there will be. Stopping the machine calls for every one of us to heal our part in the story. By awakening to a higher consciousness, we no longer engage in behaviours of lifestyles that serve the current system and instead we develop the blueprints for the new humanity where love and peace will prevail.

Many of us may wonder how can we possibly have been cheated and manipulated on such a grand scale. Surely the leaders, bankers and corporations would not put our planet at risk, threatening the wellbeing of our children and subsequent generations. For many, this is such a big thing to consider, it is impossible to take it on as truth. However our healing and enlightenment calls for us to recognise the betrayal, see what the leaders are doing, heal the discomfort and fear, move into our own space of inner empowerment and bring about change from within. It is because so many of us are unable to see the true agendas of the elite and the corporations, that they have been able to get away with so much for so long.

Freeing ourselves from the system of control and fear and leaving the so called 'rat race' brings about the possibility of a much richer experience of life, where we can experience more love and true abundance in our lives. Abundance is not about big houses and high paying jobs, but true abundance comes from within, when the heart is open we are rewarded with the flowering of love in our lives, the guidance of the Higher Beings and the awakening of spiritual wisdom. When we access this inner abundance - a sign of the awakening of the heart, then we draw into our lives much healing. Carrying the blueprint for a more loving and civilized humanity, we become guides to others, so they too may find fulfilment and meaning. In this way, more of us awaken and embrace love and the age of fear, confusion and suffering for humanity draws ever nearer to a close.

Chapter 14

Plant Teachers and Healing

There exist a number of plants on this planet with profound healing properties and these plant medicines can assist us on our healing journey. These plants are known as entheogenic, in that they awaken us to our divine nature. These medicines cannot bring us enlightenment or liberation directly - that is something we have to do for ourselves, but what they can do is allow us to journey into the subconscious realms and revisit those aspects of ourselves in deep fear and in need of healing. They can also allow us to access buried traumas from childhood and in the right setting, these medicines allow the potential for these wounded aspects of ourselves to be healed.

The Star Beings have communicated that these plants have been seeded by them, specifically to assist humanity in the transformation of consciousness. These plants also originate not from Earth but from other planets, with the psilocybin mushrooms having originated through panspermia (spores travelling through space on comets) and the ayahuasca components were placed on Earth millennia ago by the Higher Intelligences with the intention they would be discovered later by humanity.

The mainstream considers these medicines harmful, and the authorities have gone to great lengths to prohibit or restrict the use of these sacraments, with some people now serving jail sentences for possession of what are potentially the most healing medicines known to humanity. At the same time alcohol and tobacco are legal, despite causing much suffering, sickness and death on a large scale. The situation of persecution and prosecution has arisen because the authorities are deeply afraid of the potential for these medicines to assist the awakening and healing of humanity. For to heal is to see through the illusion and the world economic system that supports the elite would be seen as a sham – and it would be game over for the ruling powers and the corporations.

It is interesting to note that the love and peace consciousness that flowered in the sixties was partly due to the use of the entheogens, and the authorities stepped in quickly to suppress what was a culture of love, peace and transformation. However this consciousness is resurfacing in humanity on a much wider scale and this consciousness is also attainable without entheogens, for many other healing modalities exist in the New Age movement that enable the healing of fear and trauma. The development of love and compassion toward oneself and others can also be brought about through meditation.

I do not advocate illegal activities, and in the writing of this chapter encourage people who feel drawn to using entheogens to travel to other parts of the world where these sacraments are legal to use. The legality of some of them are also currently in question and under review, and things are subject to change, so readers are advised to become fully familiar with the laws in ones country of residence, before deciding whether to use an entheogen. It is also important to distinguish entheogenic plants such as ayahuasca, psilocybin mushrooms and peyote cactus from more recreational substances such as LSD, ecstasy and marijuana which have less spiritual value. The use of an entheogen in a recreational setting such as a nightclub is certainly not recommended, for these are very spiritual medicines that take one into a sacred space where healing can occur. Although I believe there is a strong case for legalising some of the entheogens, at the same time there is a need for discernment around how and when to use these medicines, for these medicines can be abused in the wrong context.

The information circulated by the authorities portrays the picture that these medicines can lead to temporary insanity or hallucinations and create a fear of them that is unwarranted. Conventional science does not yet understand the healing processes that these medicines can bring about, for conventional science is based on a reality that excludes the spiritual, emotional and metaphysical aspects of our being. These medicines can trigger difficult experiences, but they should not be blamed on the medicine, for the underlying cause is invariably an unresolved fear or trauma and in a proper ceremonial setting with skilled shamans these traumas can be healed. Difficulties that persist after use of the medicine, are often related to the pain of processing a buried trauma, and if proper support systems were in place for these people, rather than being labelled as mentally ill they could receive profound and deep healing.

It is important to also realise these medicines are not a replacement for spiritual practice and personal development. Rather they can be an adjunct for some peoples healing processes and when the experiences are properly integrated and grounded, these medicines are a valuable tool for self-development. It is widely believed that the medicines take one to other dimensions, however the dimensions already exist in one's own being and they simply clear away the obstacles to the higher consciousness. Meditation can also be used to achieve a similar result.

There are two main entheogens I would like to discuss in this chapter in more detail, and they are psilocybin and ayahuasca. I will not discuss LSD in depth, as it has been chemically synthesised, is harsh on the body and spirit, resulting in lengthy fatigue after use and is often tainted with toxic strychnine – a cardiovascular and muscular toxin, hence I do not advocate the use of LSD for anyone. Anything that is chemically synthesised is not natural, and only those entheogens that occur naturally have deep healing properties.

Psilocybin exists in numerous species of mushrooms, both in the UK and elsewhere. It is necessary to have expert advice before harvesting mushrooms from the wild, for there are similar looking mushrooms that can be toxic and picking random mushrooms is not recommended, for some are fatal if ingested. Psilocybin teaches us about the wisdom of connecting to nature, and helps to purify our heart of impediments to love. Species naturally occurring in the UK are mild, and the most benefit can be derived from the use of *Psilocybe Mexicana or Psilocybe Cubensis* containing much higher concentrations of psilocybin. Bear in mind that possession of fresh psilocybin mushrooms is now illegal in the UK (since 2005).

For me the use of psilocybin back in 2003, instigated a two year period of intense self-enquiry into the nature of reality and led me eventually to take up meditation so as to seek some more lasting answers. With spiritual grounding and a high enough vibration, most of what is seen can then be integrated easily. For me the experience showed me the reality of reincarnation and the ability to review one's life outside of the ego-self. It also brought about a deep ethical sensitivity, as in a life review one often feels remorse for some actions. In this light, any medicine that can help us develop ethical sensitivity has a value in the healing of humanity.

It also enabled me to transcend the ego and have some experience of other realms. Ultimately a deep exploration of these realms can only come about through deep physical, emotional and pineal detoxification, however the mushrooms were useful in that they gave me a glimpse of what was possible. Then I found it was necessary to do a long period of spiritual work so as to assimilate the experience, and pave the way for conscious access to these realms without the entheogen - which is the ultimate aim. The entheogens facilitate a cleansing of the gates of perception and allow one to move deeper into the heart, bringing about emotional healing and a deepening sensitivity. The account of my experience in 2003 was written hours after the event, and for the benefit of the reader the notes are reproduced here, to give some insights into the nature of a psilocybin experience;-

At around 7pm on the 23rd August 2003 I prepared, and drank a tea with about 20 grams of fresh Mexican Psilocybin mushrooms (legal to buy from alternative shops at the time). Within minutes marked effects occurred as I walked across a field and suddenly there was an intense feeling of changed perception, of vastness- a feeling of remembering - of coming home to the spiritual state.

Consciousness became very expanded and fluidic and seemed to extend far beyond the body, merging with trees far away. There were blades of grass everywhere, thick ones looking like some kind of crop - I sensed each one as a living being- there were millions of them. I sensed all of experience as countless energy filaments, glowing with their own inner radiance. Sometime later I felt at one with the surroundings as I had the revelation that there is no separation between experience and experiencer. There was just experience and I was part of that, not separate from the universe. Everything became one. As the ego began to dissolve, I had the revelation that the mushroom is a tool for seeing this.

Colours were strongly enhanced and walking along a road there were geometric patterns splayed out in my field of vision. I felt the fragmentation of the ego self. The self had split into a myriad of different facets. It was possible to get drawn down any one of a number of lines of thought and then to suddenly forget where you were and I had to either try and remember who I was again, or surrender into the egoless realms beyond all notions of self.

My field of vision contained coloured lights and more geometric patterns though I felt the patterns had little relevance they are just a side effect of the mushroom. The ego self became further fragmented- during the psychedelic experience one can get drawn into any one of the fragments or move into the realms of the spirit. Some of the fragments were negative, conflicting with other parts, trying to resist being fragmented. Resisting the flow of the experience created negative vibe and fear, letting go and opening one heart created bliss. Then there was a feeling

of love everywhere, it was like falling in love but many times more profound and beautiful.

I felt a deep communion with the spirit, other people would say communion with God, with the divine- it is all the same thing. With my eyes closed I saw pure gold and yellow light radiating from within. With eyes open every-thing had an added depth with objects seeming transpar-ent and appearing to break up into patterns. Everything was iridescent.

I underwent a life review, looking over some of my life. I felt I was right outside of my ordinary life on earth. I was not part of it. I was in the realms of the spirit and pure love and cosmic bliss were flowing right through me. There were moments of the ego trying to resist. I felt drawn toward a negative state – one of extreme fear. I managed to avert it. I sensed realms of fear and terror. I sensed a hell realm which is self created by shutting off from universal love and getting trapped in guilt circles .I did not go there either. I had a sense of being beyond physical life and in the realm of the afterlife. I had a sense of death being just a stage in the process of life and not the end. I was reviewing my life from some external standpoint.

Then in another vision I was beyond the earth merging out into the universe- and I had a very brief vision of a species from another planet- extraterrestrial life and a spacecraft. I felt I had an option to plunge deep into the universe with them but I did not take it.
Intense feelings of cosmic love arose and with eyes closed I saw myself on a mountain. Then I entered a stage of what I would describe as a spiritual overhaul. I was re-

evaluating who I was. For a brief moment I saw that all of physical matter and the self as an illusion.

There was still a lot of gold colour in the consciousness-with eyes open or closed. With them closed I saw faces in the midst of it. I had a sense of hundreds of beings merging with the universe in a state of cosmic love, inviting me to join. I saw myself create a barrier around me. Suddenly I got anxious and scared – I then realized I was resisting the flow of the experience and closing off to universal love. I relaxed and the bliss returned. I just lay there in the bliss for some time sensing universal love everywhere.

The experience started to subside and normality returned swiftly. An hour later there was not a single remnant of the altered state remaining. But there was a deep awareness of having seen beyond this life and this plane. All in all it was a very deep spiritual experience, a very profound one that I will remember for a while.

For me, the above experience helped me to re-evaluate my identity in a very positive way. I was able to understand the nature of ego in a way I may not have otherwise been able to without the psilocybin teacher. It also brought about a profound awakening of heart and a deep love for nature, which then inspired me to start a recycling project and to plant over 1000 trees in the following years. Most importantly, it brought about a transformation of heart, and was beneficial in instigating a deep emotional healing process. The entheogens show us deeper aspects of ourselves that we may otherwise never discover. Even though at times the experience was frightening, in the end the outcome was very positive. It is this buried fear that we all need to heal now, and the psilocybin is one method where these fears can be brought to the surface in a sacramental and loving context. The spirit of the mushroom is ultimately a sentient, loving, intelligent teacher that nurtures, guides and heals.

Ayahuasca is another healing medicine which is a combination of two plants from the Amazon rainforest that contain naturally occurring DMT molecules. The plant material, a vine and a leaf, are boiled in large pots by shamans for many hours, whilst chanting is done to infuse the mixture with the vibration of the Divine. The result is a thick brown liquid that tastes incredibly bitter and is very challenging to drink. Ayahuasca is not for everyone, simply because the effects are so strong.

However for those able to handle the medicine, deep bodily and emotional healing is possible. The medicine is known in some countries as 'La Purga', for in many people it induces intense vomiting as the medicine clears the body of toxins. This toxic clearing paves the way for the medicine to heal on a deeper level. For some reason, despite having drunk ayahuasca on many occasions, I have never vomited. It may be down to the raw foods diet, and because I do not vomit the medicine is totally absorbed and assimilated. The spiritual essence of the ayahuasca is then not lost which may have contributed to a sense of long term inner illumination and the ability to communicate with higher dimensional beings on a daily basis.

Invariably the ingestion of ayahuasca will bring one in touch with the most wounded aspects of oneself and so one can find oneself undergoing a very difficult passage as past traumas are relived. However, ultimately this is a very beneficial process and many people report profound healing from the use of ayahuasca. My experience of the medicine initially was of experiencing deep fear from within with no obvious cause. Later work with the medicine revealed a wounded two year old inner child, and I was then able to work with this trauma and bring about a complete healing where all the fear was released. All the energy the fear had drained from me was returned, revitalising my life with clarity, purpose and confidence, and enhancing my ability to love. For childhood wounds prevent us from being able to love and through the loving guidance of the ayahuasca, we can find release from our childhood dramas, and be remade in heart and spirit. The ayahuasca can enable one to become strong and fearless, yet gentle and loving.

With ayahuasca we can also contact the spirits of nature and we can have visionary experiences of all kinds of creatures, with hummingbirds, tigers and serpents being the most common. Ayahuasca is a strong teacher, shows us things as they are and holds nothing back. Hidden wounds, old karmas and subconscious power games all come into awareness in the presence of ayahuasca, giving an opportunity for massive transformation. Ayahuasca teaches us how to live with humility, compassion and reverence for all that lives. It shows us how to bring our lives back into alignment with sacredness and love, and all who use the medicine find transformation in heart and spirit. The ability of this medicine to heal humanity should not be underestimated. Unfortunately however, this medicine is a banned substance in many countries.

This sacrament has come out from the rainforest at this time because it carries so much healing potential for humanity today. The dynamics in modern society that prohibit the use of such natural sacraments will need to be healed and transformed, so that people are given free choice as to whether they wish to use these naturally occurring medicines without state intervention or control.

It has been thought for some time that there may be some medicines in the rainforest with abilities to heal cancer and other human afflictions that we may lose because of the destruction of the rainforest. I believe Ayahuasca is one of these valuable medicines, and fortunately has been brought out of the rainforest just in time and is now more accessible to humanity. When the value of this medicine is understood by the human collective, it is likely we will reverse deforestation, heal our connection to nature and make other valuable natural discoveries in the Amazon that can heal us. Ultimately the plant medicines from the Amazon heal us of our separation from love and nature, and thus give the potential for humanity to heal our destructive tendencies, save the rainforest, and ourselves from environmental disaster.

The interesting thing about DMT (the active component of ayahuasca) is that the human pineal gland will manufacture large amounts of it and release it into the bloodstream at the time of death. It is my belief that the presence of DMT in the body will facilitate the seeing of the afterlife dimension, and thus it is a valuable ally in understanding the death process whilst alive. The experience of using ayahuasca can sometimes bring about a passage through the different bardos (realms) of existence (as outlined in the Tibetan Book of the Dead) and so can offer some preparation for navigating the afterlife dimension when our death comes.

If the pineal gland is fully functional and the body receives optimum nutrition the pineal gland will also begin releasing DMT into the body throughout one's life without the use of ayahuasca, precipitating the awakening of dormant spiritual abilities such as lucid dreaming, astral travel, ESP, premonition and telepathy. This is a totally natural process and I believe that the ingestion of environmental toxins has shut down the pineal gland in the majority of individuals and stopped this process, resulting in loss of our higher brain functions.

The new humanity will recognise the value of these plant medicines in healing the body, heart and spirit. It is likely they will become part of our culture in the coming years, available freely for those people who wish to follow this path to healing. It is vital now, at this time of global crisis, for the misconceptions around these plant medicines to be resolved. It is very likely the authorities know that these medicines can facilitate spiritual awakening and this is most likely the reason why they are so restricted. Once the current political structure has been replaced these medicines will be properly understood and free from prohibition they will play their part in the healing of humanity.

Chapter 15

Spiritual perspectives and reflections

The heart of humanity is now suffering and lacking love whilst all of our karmas and unresolved issues are rising to the surface for resolution. The next decade or so is likely to prove a very difficult passage for humanity. However difficult the transition may seem, it is worth reflecting on the fact that whatever happens is for our higher evolutionary purpose. As love is the principle vibration of the Universe, then all suffering has a spiritual purpose in restoring us to that place of love. Often it is only through suffering that we are forced to face ourselves, those wounded parts of ourselves we would otherwise not face, and to see through the illusions that otherwise we choose to go along with. After we have been through the passage of suffering, our hearts become purified. Free from sorrow, we feel only love and our actions reflect our inner state of love, kindness and compassion. We can then assist others to lift their vibration by demonstrating love and compassion to others still suffering and showing them the way out of it.

Suffering is always a spiritually transforming experience and is not a random affliction handed down to us by a judgemental God or Higher Being. If we meditate and reflect deeply, we will realise that our individual and collective suffering is purely caused by our thoughts and actions. When we realise this deeply, we become empowered, masters of our own destiny and then develop the awareness and ability to rise out of suffering. Human suffering seems an immense problem with no immediate resolution - however it is not something we have to experience and is limited to this dimension only, for in all my journeys into the higher realms, I have only ever found love, light, healing, and the total absence of suffering.

Though reflection and spiritual work, all of the causes of suffering can be understood and thus resolved. Attempting to eliminate suffering without having the courage to face the underlying cause will achieve little. Healing from suffering comes through facing oneself and finding courage to overcome the fear of doing so. Often we are afraid to look at ourselves because of what we may find – a wounded true self, and instead we create the illusion of a false self (the mask) to cover the wounds and then draw into our lives further anguish and suffering.

The end of suffering can only come when we recognise and embody spiritual truth, and transcend fear. The truth is that there is an abundance of love in the higher planes and a much wiser, more enlightened state of consciousness awaits those who can make the passage out of fear. Fear and love cannot exist simultaneously, so the moment we choose the path of love, our fear diminishes. Almost every kind of suffering imaginable will have a root cause in fear and at some point in our past because of some difficult experience we will have moved away from love. It is the return to the heart that cleanses the soul of all troubles and awakens us to the freshness and wonder of the higher dimensions. In this space we can absorb and be nourished by the spiritual light, whilst feeling very loved and nurtured by the Higher Intelligences.

Love is very powerful in that when it is fully embodied, it gives us many abilities to face all kinds of difficult situations, and thus it is love that has the ability to carry humanity through the challenging passages into the new consciousness. In a space of love, we are open to and can receive all kinds of guidance from the Higher Beings that can help us to transcend our ego-created illusions and awaken to our deeper nature. It is the absence of love from the heart of humanity that has created the situation humanity is in now and so it is by beginning the journey back to heart we can begin to unravel the numerous causes that has brought humanity into crisis. Many global problems today, when reflected upon, have a root cause in a lack of love.

In the new humanity, there will be not competition but co-operation. When six billion people are attempting to compete with and outwit one another to become more successful, or earn more money, it is impossible for there to be any unity built on common purpose. In that mind-set, the importance of love is forgotten, human relation-ships suffer and conflict develops. Confusion and fear follow when we become separated from love. Today the purpose of many is simply to amass wealth and the monetary systems perpetuate separation, domination, consumption and lack of co-operation.

There will be a time in the not too distant future where all of humanity will have a common purpose and all the resources of the planet will be used responsibly and pooled for the benefit of all. As fully healed human beings we will have moved past greed and the desire to hoard, and so we will only take what we need from the Earth. In a state of love, we will also give and contribute what we can to humanity so all is in balance, and we will never take more from the Earth than that which nature can afford to give.

For those attached to stories of control, domination and greed their days on this planet are coming to an end. They are karmically destined to leave the Earth to allow the rest of humanity to come together in love and common purpose. With their passage of suffering through death or intense healing completed, humanity will become purified, with love finally becoming the unifying and driving force behind the further evolution of humanity.

Love is so much needed now, for our emotional capacity will need to be greatly expanded to be able to function during the transitions. If we are not firmly rooted in a space of love, then when the old systems collapse we face the danger of succumbing to fear, and in those spaces we can act irrationally and cause harm to others, and bringing to ourselves further suffering. Surviving the transitions will be most likely by those who have transcended fear, and who are   loving human beings. As I have said before, there will be no apocalypse, but there will be a collapse of the old systems and an ensuing chaos, for these systems are not based on love, and thus will not be able to support the expansion of consciousness now arising in so many of us.

It is important now for all of us to face the situation humanity is in, rather than shrinking away in fear. Often we do not wish to face the bigger issues, but this is exactly what is asked of us now. When we have the courage to do so, we heal our own part of the story in the process until a day will come when even though humanity faces a difficult passage, one stands strong, fearless and unshaken and accepts everything as it is. Free from fear, one knows only love and in that space, one can achieve much and be of great assistance to others in the coming transitions.

Hiding in our fears will do nothing but delay our healing and increase our suffering. We owe it to ourselves and to humanity now to come out of our ego-created comfort zones that give us a false sense of security, to face ourselves and bring about the final transformation of ourselves and our planet. The longer we remain in denial, the more difficult it will be for humanity to heal itself, as multiple issues will present themselves for resolution with little warning. If we can find courage to really see the situation we are in, then we can change it and the outcome can be more positive - for us individually and for the collective. We create our own reality through our thoughts and level of consciousness, so any positive inner changes will be reflected back to us in the outer world.

There is great hope for humanity now as many of us are beginning to embrace a new consciousness whilst seeing there is a way out of our suffering and difficulties. As we embrace love we also begin to receive the assistance from the Star Beings. Their love can lift us into joyous realms of vibration, in alignment with the light we can create a new reality where love is seen as important and the eradication of suffering becomes the primary aim of humanity. In a space of love, we will help those in need, no-one will go hungry whilst others consume too much and we will also love nature and the animals. Communities will prosper, families will come together and all the wounds caused by separation will be healed. Spiritual peace will be restored amongst humankind.

Chapter 16

Closing
Messages
A call to action

This is a time of great change and many things are possible. Lay down your fears and heal your hearts so you may become strong and stand in the light. Do not fear the coming of the Star Beings, for they come to show the way for humanity.

They bring with them the gift of love and if we are open to receiving it we can be purified of all suffering. Do not allow your fears and doubts to hold you back from walking fully into the light. Leave them behind and never will you suffer or be separated from love again.

This is the age when the spiritual truths will be reincarnated into your species so that all may be transformed and healed. Then humanity can avoid its demise and instead make it to the stars and experience the full wonders of the multidimensional universe. Millions of unexplored worlds await humanity and a vast number of loving intelligences spread across the entire galaxy are open to relationship with us as humanity turns toward the stars.

Now is the time to give up one's attachments to conventions and material ideals for they will bring you nothing but death. They will not accompany humanity on this journey into a more enlightened age. The things that will count in the coming transitions will be love, compassion, spiritual understanding, physical health and the ability to surrender your attachments to almost everything you have considered truth, for the new realities are about to be unveiled to you.

Renounce all violence and other crimes against your fellow people, for all are one and of the same Source. Instead turn to your fellow humans and practice love, compassion and forgiveness, and build communities based on these values. Do not let the rulers of the planet control you by playing on your fears. Whatever happens in the world, whatever dramas play out, continue undisturbed on your path of healing and spreading love.

Cleanse your body of the toxic metals, pesticides and chemicals, and cleanse your heart of your old hurts. Then one day you will become aware of the communications of the Star Beings. They speak to you in dreams and through intuition, prior to their arrival on Earth. Look deeply within and explore your consciousness and you will find them – ambassadors of love and light from the higher planes – they guide your way back to the Source and offer you the possibility of enlightenment and the transcendence of the human condition.

Know that love can heal everything and make anything possible. If you find anything that prevents you from loving, then work with it until you can love. For the heart is the doorway into the new age of humanity.

Peace and love be in your hearts always.

Free Spirit

Glossary

Alpha Centauri – One of the nearest stars to our Solar System, at approximately 4 light years distant. Part of a triple star system.

Ascension – A shift in conscious vibration upwards, whilst incorporating new realities. For example, the ascension out of suffering into spaces of love and light.

Ascension can also refer to movement out of the matter plane, and a subsequent departure from the Earth through the use of a star gate, multidimensional star-craft or through transmutation of the physical body into light.

Astral planes - Non physical dimensions of existence immediately above our own where we find ourselves after death. These realms can also be explored by the light body during sleep.

Aura – Electromagnetic energy surrounding our physical bodies, taking on the form of a light halo. Its size depends on the vitality and wellbeing of the person concerned.

Ayahuasca - Shamanic plant medicine from the Amazonian rainforest, containing DMT which activates the pineal gland and purges the body of toxins.

Benevolent - Meaning no harm. Benevolent beings come with positive agendas and the healing of humanity in mind.

Brane - A higher dimensional membrane existing within hyperspace acting as a boundary between different dimensions. They can be likened to the surface of a bubble.

Chakras - Energy centres of the body or the Earth. The human body has seven. They channel the life force energy from the higher planes into the physical form, and can be visualised as coloured spinning wheels or spirals.

Crown chakra - The chakra above the top of the head that facilitates illumination and the influx of energy from the higher dimensions.

DNA - The building blocks of life, containing the genetic instructions for the creation of new cells. Physical DNA takes the form of a double helix, however there are additional strands of spiritual light based DNA not visible under the microscope, responsible for the reawakening of our dormant light bodies.

Ego death - An experience where the ego (illusory notion of self) is temporarily dissolved resulting in an awareness of spiritual reality beyond the self.

Ethereal - Consisting of spiritual light / astral matter.

Galactic Core – The centre of our galaxy – 30,000 light years from Earth and which exists across several dimensions. It is the entry point for higher dimensional energy into our galaxy.

Great Central Sun – A huge white star at the centre of the galaxy, billions of times the size of our own Sun and existing in a higher dimension. It appears as a black hole in this reality, but is a white hole when seen from the spiritual planes. It is the portal for transit of souls in and out of this galaxy.

Heavy metals - Dense, toxic metals such as cadmium and mercury that have no place in the human body and impede the ascension process.

Hyperspace - The overall container for higher dimensional realities, existing beyond the confines of time and ordinary spatial notions.

Hypercube - A cube existing in four or more dimensions.

Hypersphere - A sphere existing in four or more dimensions. Hyperspheres of varying complexity can be created by the Star Beings and used as crafts to achieve trans-dimensional travel.

Immortalisation - The transcendence of death by drawing all the higher dimensional vibrations into the physical body, which brings about a union of the physical and spiritual dualities. The physical body becomes transmuted into light, and is freed of physical plane laws, and one becomes immortal.

Inner luminosity - The inner light nature of any sentient being. Made of higher dimensional light vibrations, and is the only aspect of ourselves that is immortal and ultimately real.

Karma - The law of cause and effect. Previous actions, either good or bad create karmic consequences that must be experienced later. All actions leave energetic residues in one's being that lie dormant until external circumstances trigger fruition.

Kundalini - The main channel for light energy linking all the chakras from above the head to the base of the body.

Law of One - The spiritual truth and reality of non-duality and interconnectedness.

Leylines - Energy channels within the Earths auric grid.

Light Beings - Higher dimensional beings without physical bodies, and includes Star Beings, angels, nature spirits and other etheric intelligences.

LSD - Lysergic acid diethylamide. A synthetic psychedelic substance derived from ergot which causes shifts in consciousness and perception, and can induce religious or mystical experience.

Matrices - Higher dimensional energy grids.

Nexus – A hub.

Orbs - A higher dimensional phenomena – made from light, and have the ability to appear and disappear at will, as well as fly at high speed across the sky. They can also move through matter and sometimes appear to have faces.

Pineal gland - A gland within the brain responsible for spiritual perception and awakening.

Portal - A gateway to another dimension - either natural or created by Higher Intelligences. Created ones are often known as **Star gates**.

Psilocybin - The active component of several mushroom species that can induce spiritual experiences when ingested.

Rainbow Key - A vibrational tool given by the Star Beings which raises the vibration of the aura to a level that permits portal travel. It also permits perception of the rainbow realms of light existing beyond the fifth dimension.

Ra-Collective - A collective of Star Beings on the 9th dimension, from which most of the channelled information in this book originates.

Ra-Homeworld - A 9th dimensional blue star, the home of the **Ra-Collective**.

Source - The origin of our spirit essence and of higher dimensional energies – the **Galactic Core**.

Star gate - A portal to dimensions beyond the Earth plane, permitting instantaneous passage to other Solar Systems across the galaxy. Some are naturally occurring planetary vortices, and others are created by the Star Beings.

Starseed consciousness - The awareness of cosmic consciousness along with the remembrance of one's cosmic origins, life purpose and relationships with Star Beings.

Transmutation - In the context of this book, the conversion of the physical body into non-physical, ethereal light form.

About the author

Free Spirit changed his name by deed poll in 2004 when he was 29 after having a series of spiritual experiences in the Himalayas, and a growing sense of disillusionment with conventional, materialistic life.

In 2008, he studied Environmental Sciences at the Open University for 1 year and gained a Distinction.

After understanding deeply the predicament humanity is in, he saw how academic study had little value in the healing of humanity and so left his studies.

In 2009, he began to experience contact with the Star Beings and took up public speaking and writing so as to share his experiences of deep healing and to communicate the messages for humanity from them.

He has a website – www.awakening2012.co.uk, selling high vibrational superfoods and communicating the messages from the Star Beings.

He is available to give talks and lectures worldwide, and to speak to the media if asked.

CPSIA information can be obtained at www.ICGtesting.com
Printed in the USA
LVOW102130190912

299555LV00014B/13/P